32290

E
99
C24
H8

Hudson, C

The Catawba Nation

DATE DUE			

j

UNIVERSITY OF GEORGIA MONOGRAPHS, NO. 18

The Catawba Nation

By

CHARLES M. HUDSON
DEPARTMENT OF SOCIOLOGY AND ANTHROPOLOGY
UNIVERSITY OF GEORGIA

UNIVERSITY OF GEORGIA PRESS

ATHENS   1970

For

CHARLIE and ANN REBECCA

Copyright © 1970
University of Georgia Press
LC 75-119554
SBN 8203-0255-4

Printed in the United States

iv

Contents

Preface

My task has been to reconstruct the history of the Catawba Indians, concentrating on the history of their external relations, and to examine the manner in which this history is remembered and socially codified in the present. As a piece of ethnohistorical research, such a study is somewhat novel, but it conforms to a recent trend in social anthropology. That is, social anthropologists increasingly insist that we must not only describe and document exotic societies in *our* terms but in *their* terms as well; we must not only examine the variability of social action but also the categories by which men reduce their social environment to manageable proportions.

Putting it another way, perhaps the most important task of social anthropology is to investigate, in concrete cases, the links between believed-in states of affairs (categories) and observed, acted-out states of affairs (social action); but the links between believed-in history and actual history—that is, "actual" insofar as we can determine it—are also of considerable theoretical importance. The notion that society has a real "synchronic" existence has been profoundly beneficial in the development of the social sciences generally; without this, we would never have wrested our identity from the "diachronic" historical sciences. But society as a synchronic entity is something of a fiction; society does, in fact, have an extension into the past. We have seen this dramatically in our own time in the controversy over William Manchester's *The Death of a President*. The assassination of John Kennedy was an historical fact, but the details of his last days in office and his assassination were still relevant to the period in which Manchester wrote, else there would have been no controversy. A moment's reflection shows that people distinguish "we" and "they" not only in the present but also in their own social past, assigning "they" to remote ancestors, and the point at which this distinction is made of considerable theoretical importance. It demarcates the temporal extension of a society into its past, and it is obvious that this demarcation is of great importance in any assessment of social change.

Although this book includes a history of the Catawba Indians, it is not meant to replace books like Douglas Summers Brown's *Catawba Indians,* and although it contains firsthand ethnographic material, it is not meant to be a community study, nor does it attempt to depict the Catawba Indians "in the round." The main effort, instead, is interpretative and theoretical. What anthropology needs is a framework of theoretical ideas that takes account of both the temporal and atemporal dimensions of social life, for an exaggerated methodological distinction between temporal and atemporal, diachronic and synchronic, does violence to what anthropologists observe and try to describe. Furthermore, this theoretical framework should be sensitive to both the standardized and the unique; it should emphasize the interplay between the two. It is the experience of everyone that many social events and actions do not accord with ideals, values, or expectations. Social events are inevitably a combination of the standardized and the unique. Whatever the particulars of such a theoretical framework, it must take full account of a fundamental paradox in human experience: even though we may know that all events are unique, we must act as if they are not.

In keeping with the dual nature of this inquiry, the methods I have used are also dual, being a mixture of historiography and ethnography. The pages that follow are thus based both on library research and field research. The chapters dealing with the early history of the Catawbas are almost exclusively based on library research. Both library and field research went into the chapters dealing with the later history of the Catawbas. The chapter devoted to the folk history of the Catawbas is primarily based on field research.

My field notes come from two short periods of field work. The first period lasted from the first of August until the middle of September 1962. In terms of concrete results, this period of field work was a mere beginning; it was, however, valuable in two ways. I succeeded in establishing rapport with several Catawbas, and on the basis of the information they gave me, I was able to formulate a clearer picture of the research problem. Initially I planned to do a synchronic study, but after analyzing initial data I became convinced that there were problems in the research that would not yield to a synchronic analysis.

Before beginning the second period of field work, I reformulated the problem in approximately the form discussed above. This second period of field work lasted from the first of June until the middle of October 1963. Since the object of this field work was to learn how the Catawbas and their white neighbors thought of themselves in terms of their past, I felt that a mixture of directed interviewing and participant-observation would be the most appropriate means of acquiring this information. I consistently defined my role as that of a student of Catawba history. There were some initial difficulties in persuading everybody to accept this, but I feel that most of the people eventually accepted it as a satisfactory explanation of my actions.

My greatest debts are to John J. Honigmann, who supported my field work with a grant (MH 06903-01) from the National Institute of Mental Health and who guided my research in important ways; to the National Institute of Mental Health for a Predoctoral Fellowship (1 F1-MH 19, 858-01) while I analyzed my data and wrote it up in the form of a Ph.D. dissertation; and to Peter Carstens for invaluable advice and encouragement. I am also grateful to William S. Pollitzer, Joffre L. Coe, Gerhard Lenski, Richard Lieban, William Sturtevant, and William Dunning.

The historical parts of this book have gained much from the help given me by Lauritz Pederson and A. William Lund of the Latter-day Saints Library in Salt Lake City, Utah, and I owe an even greater debt to Mrs. Nan Carson, librarian of the Public Library in Rock Hill, South Carolina. I also want to thank Louis DeVorsey for giving me the benefit of his knowledge of early maps of the Southeast and James Barnes for cartographic help.

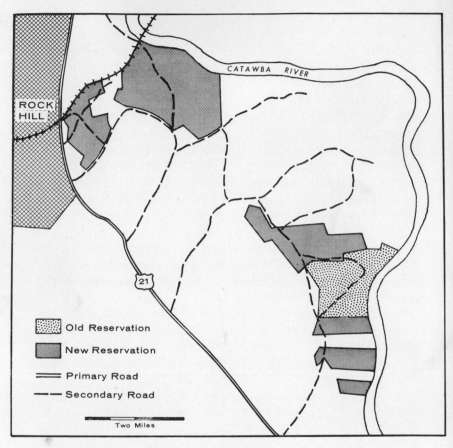

MAP 1. OLD AND NEW CATAWBA RESERVATIONS.

CHAPTER I

Forms of Catawba History

THE majority of people known as Catawba Indians live in the state of South Carolina. According to their final tribal membership roll, by their own count they were 631 in number on July 2, 1960 (Carver 1961). Some of these live eight miles southeast of the city of Rock Hill on the "Old Reservation." This tract of land, a tiny fraction of their original territory, is still held in trust by South Carolina. Other Catawbas live in the immediate vicinity of the Old Reservation on lands that until recently were called the "New Reservation." Acquired in 1943, these lands were administered by the Bureau of Indian Affairs until the Catawbas chose to terminate their relationship with the Bureau in 1962. However, even though the Catawbas at that time ceased to be Indians in the eyes of the Federal government, white people in Rock Hill still occasionally refer to the Catawbas and their reservation as the "Nation," a designation that has enjoyed meaningful usage for over two and a half centuries.

Our fullest early description of the Catawbas comes to us from the hand of John Lawson, who visited them in January 1701 while on a journey from Charleston, South Carolina, to the mouth of the Tar River in North Carolina (Lawson 1960:29-41). Having made contact with the Sewee, Santee, Congaree, and Wateree Nations while traveling on foot up the eastern banks of the Santee-Wateree-Catawba River system, he came upon the Catawba Nation situated a few miles from the present day Old Reservation.[1] The Waxhaw,

1. For consistency, I have adopted the spellings of Indian names used by James Mooney in his *Siouan Tribes of the East*.

1

Esaw, and Sugeree Nations were situated near the Catawba
Nation, and all four appear to have been closely related.
Regrettably, Lawson says very little that applies specifically
to the Catawbas, but his description of the Waxhaws is
probably representative of the Catawbas as well.

Upon arriving among the Waxhaws, Lawson was enter-
tained in a "cabin" that impressed him as being unusually
large and well built. The Indians of all four nations lived in
villages scattered through an area at least ten miles across.
Each village had a "theatre" or "stagehouse" that was larger
in size and different in construction from the bark-covered
houses in which they lived. In these public buildings, am-
bassadors from other nations were received, political affairs
were deliberated, and rituals were performed. Each village
apparently had a governing council of elders with a presiding
"king" and "war-captain," the relationships among these
being governed by a precise code of etiquette. At the time
of Lawson's visit, an ambassador was present from the Saponi
Nation, located over 150 miles to the north.

Lawson was later invited into one of the state-houses where
he and his hosts feasted on "Loblolly and other Medleys, made
of Indian Grain, Stewed peaches, Bear-Venison, &c."

Presently in came fine Men dressed up with feathers, their
faces being covered with Vizards made of Gourds; round their
Ancles [sic] and Knees were hung Bells of several sorts;
having Wooden Falchions in their Hands, (such as Stage-Fencers
commonly used); in this Dress they danced about an Hour, showing many strange Gestures, and brandishing their Wooden
Weapons as if they were going to fight each other; oftentimes
walking very nimbly round the Room, without making the
least Noise with their Bells, (a thing I much admired at). . . .

When the festivities ended there was a period of sexual
license, when "every Youth that was so disposed, catched hold
of the Girl he liked best, and took her that Night for his
Bed-Fellow, making as short Courtship and expeditious Wed-
ding, as the Foot-Guards used to do with the Trulls in
Salisbury-Court" (1960:34-36).

Let us now span two and a half centuries to look briefly
at the Catawba Nation that may be seen by modern tourists.

A few miles southeast of Rock Hill on U. S. Highway 21 to Columbia, there is a small sign which reads *Catawba Indian Reservation* with an arrow pointing rather indefinitely toward a narrow asphalt road. Tourists sometimes turn up this road in search of Indians. As they drive along the crooked road, they soon come to a similar sign pointing toward another narrow road. Following this turn, many proceed in a wide arc taking them to another intersection with Highway 21 and a third sign, identical to the first two, pointing in the direction from which they have come.

An unobservant tourist may well drive through the reservation unawares, and many do. Indeed, there is little to distinguish it from other rural neighborhoods in South Carolina. The houses range from simple structures of unpainted wood to modern brick houses resembling those in surburbia. Physically, the people living in these houses range from blondes and redheads to a few who strongly resemble the people whom Lawson visited. To a casual observer, the Catawba Indians are not markedly different in appearance from some of the groups with Indian admixture found in various parts of the eastern United States (Berry 1963). Most of the Catawbas have jobs in the textile industry, the most important enterprise in the Rock Hill economy. All of the Catawbas are monolingual English speakers; the last speaker of the Catawba language died while they were in the process of terminating their relationship with the Bureau of Indian Affairs.

Some of the tourists who drive through notice two homemade signs advertising Catawba Indian pottery. Curiously, this pottery is made by techniques similar to those in use at the time of Lawson's visit, but the forms in which the pottery is made are mostly modern. Some of the tourists are undoubtedly puzzled upon seeing a neat, carefully maintained Mormon chapel; almost all of the Catawbas (and a few whites) are Mormons. Thus modern Catawbas are distinctive in some ways, but for the most part they think and live like ordinary Americans of the Southeast.

Because of a paucity of historical data, it is not possible to reconstruct a full picture of Catawba life at the time of Lawson's visit. However, it is clear that his "Catawba Nation" referred to a social entity quite different from that existing today. Thus we see that "Catawba Nation" raises an interesting semantic problem. The name has remained the same over a period of more than 250 years, but the "things" to which it refers are so different they are scarcely comparable.

Social anthropologists have recently begun investigating the way in which people categorize and interpret the world in which they live through the use of highly general classifications, beliefs, and "theories." This is obviously a study of great importance; some would say that it is the most important task in social anthropology. It is less obvious that what is true of the present is also true of the past: people interpret their past in terms of categories just as they interpret their present, and "Catawba Nation" is one of these categories. But recognizing the admitted heuristic value of the notion of category, further explanation is needed. Granted that an historian (or anthropologist) can reconstruct the history (or ethnohistory) of a social group with some claim to objectivity, we may also ask how that social group perceives its own past. What is the nature of its "folk history" (Hudson 1966)?

The aim of this book is to give an account of both kinds of history. Chapters II through V are devoted to an ethnohistorical account of the Catawbas from prehistoric times up to the present. Chapter VI, on the other hand, is devoted to their folk history, their past as they believe it to have been. In addition, I include in chapter VI a brief description of how the local whites conceive of Catawba history. As we shall see, the white version of Catawba history is somewhat different from the Catawba's version of their own history, adding to a growing body of evidence that history is refracted by social structure in such a way that different groups in a society believe in different versions of the past (Hudson 1966). Far from being mere antiquarian pursuits, folk histories are vital parts of the stuff of social structure; were this not the case, the enormous interest in Negro history in the United States in the 1960's would make no sense.

CHAPTER II

The Ancestors of the Catawbas

THE word "Catawba" first came into usage at the beginning of the eighteenth century when it began to appear in travelers' journals and colonial records. One of the earliest uses of the word is in John Lawson's account of his travels in 1700-1701. However, there is considerable evidence that the ancestors of the people visited by Lawson were settled in the vicinity of his visit considerably before the beginning of the eighteenth century. Who were these people, and what were their cultural and social affinities?

The standard accounts of the Catawbas and related Indians are primarily based on inferential evidence. James Mooney's (1894) pioneering classification of the Catawbas as "Eastern Siouans" is purportedly based on linguistic evidence. Most of the subsequent anthropological research on the Catawbas, such as the work of John R. Swanton and Frank G. Speck, relies on Mooney rather heavily while differing in certain details. While inferential evidence is generally less reliable than direct, dated historical evidence, it is nevertheless capable of producing valuable results. However, as Sapir was careful to point out, inferential evidence must be subjected to vigorous scrutiny and methodological rigor; otherwise it can lead to a badly distorted reconstruction, particularly in the hands of someone with a "theory" (Sapir 1951:394). As we shall presently see, Mooney's reconstruction and the classification on which it is based are methodologically defective.

Toward the end of the nineteenth century anthropologists and historians had succeeded in mapping the pre-Columbian location of nominate aboriginal groups in most of the eastern

United States. The Algonquian-speaking Powhatans, who figure so prominently in early American history, were concentrated in the Virginia tidewater area. North of the Powhatans lay the Iroquoian-speaking Five Nations, a powerful and well known confederacy. To the south, the Cherokees held the southern Appalachian mountains and adjacent areas. Further south, the southern piedmont and coastal plain were dominated by Muskogean-speaking Indians, the ancestors of the historic Creeks.

However, an annoying hiatus lay between the Powhatans and the Creeks and between the Cherokees and the Atlantic coast. This area embracing the piedmont and coastal plain of the Carolinas was known to have contained a large number of poorly documented aboriginal groups; aside from their names, little was known about them. A partial answer to this puzzle came in the 1870's when Horatio Hale, a Canadian linguist, obtained a vocabulary from a Tutelo who was living with the Cayuga Indians. After analyzing his data, Hale reached the startling conclusion that the Tutelo language—originally spoken by people occupying the hiatus—was neither Muskogean, Iroquoian, nor Algonquian; it was genetically related to the Siouan languages that were previously thought to have been limited to the buffalo-hunters of the Great Plains (Hale 1883).[1] Additional Tutelo vocabularies were subsequently collected by Frachtenberg (1913) and Sapir (1913).

Confirmation for Hale's discovery came in 1881. At this time, Albert S. Gatschet gave a Catawba vocabulary to James Owen Dorsey, a Siouan specialist, who immediately identified it as a Siouan language (Gatschet 1900). On the basis of a short vocabulary of Woccon in Lawson's *History*, Albert Gallatin (1836) had previously recognized a genetic relationship between Woccon and Catawba. Thus, toward the close of the nineteenth century it appeared that at least three of the aboriginal groups in the Carolina hiatus spoke Siouan languages. Of these three languages only Catawba was reasonably well documented, the data being very scanty on both Tutelo and Woccon.

---

1. Frank T. Siebert (1945) has pointed out that Lewis H. Morgan suggested that Catawba was a Siouan language in 1869; however, Hale seems to have made his discovery independently.

Impressed by these startling linguistic correspondences, James Mooney published his influential *Siouan Tribes of the East* in 1894. Along with Catawba, Tutelo, and Woccon, Mooney concludes that twenty-six additional named groups were also "Eastern Siouans," including the Monacan, Saponi, Occaneechi, Sara, Keyauwee, Eno, Waxhaw, Sugeree, Peedee, Sewee, Santee, Wateree, and Congaree.[2] The astonishing thing about this "linguistic" classification is that aside from their names there is no direct linguistic evidence on any of these groups.

Actually, Mooney's classification is not linguistic; it is one of those "theories" that are often encountered in early studies of prehistory which seem to simplify but actually distort. On the basis of the Siouan linguistic correspondences already discussed and a knowledge of Plains ethnology, Mooney jumped to the conclusion that the Carolina hiatus was populated by people who were physically and culturally related to the colorful, nomadic Plains Indians. He further theorized that the original home of the "Siouan race" was in the eastern foothills of the southern Allegheny Mountains; here they suffered from a fairly recent southern expansion of aggressive Iroquoians, subsequently splitting into western and eastern divisions and migrating to their historic locations (Mooney 1894:9).

John R. Swanton (1936) adopts the main outlines of Mooney's classification while modifying it in several respects. One modification is that Swanton thought he saw evidence for a linguistic division among the "Eastern Siouans": a northern or Virginia division including the Manahoac, Monacan, Nahyssan, Saponi, Tutelo, Occaneechi, and Mohetan; and a southern or Carolina division including the Catawbas and their neighbors. Swanton attempted to substantiate this division by arguing that the Carolina Siouans entered their historic territory through the southern foothills of the Alleghenies, while the Virginia Siouans entered their historic territory along the Kanawha River. Like Mooney, Swanton thought that the "Eastern Siouans" mi-

---

2. The others are the Mahoc, Nuntaneuck, Mohetan, Meipontsky, Shoccoree, Adshusheer, Sissipahaw, Cape Fear, Warrennuncock, Waccamaw, Winyaw, Hooks, and Backhooks.

grated into the Carolinas and Virginia in relatively recent times.

The Eastern Siouan classification of Mooney and Swanton is, to say the least, based on very tenuous evidence. As we have already seen, there is direct evidence of Siouan linguistic identity for only three of them: Catawba, Tutelo, and Woccon. All the others are classified as Siouan on indirect evidence. For example, Mooney deduces that the Monacan and Manahoac were Siouan-speakers because William Byrd, a colonial writer, reports second- or third-hand that their languages were similar to Tutelo and Saponi (1894:23). Similarly, Swanton bases his dichotomy of Eastern Siouans into northern and southern divisions partly on the grounds that the members of these divisions tended to align themselves politically. It is possible, of course, that some of the cultures listed by Mooney and Swanton spoke Siouan languages, but linguistic classification must be based on linguistic evidence. The political alliances of eastern Indians, particularly when European pressure became severe, are poor indices of linguistic affinity. Some Tutelos, for example, who spoke a Siouan language, eventually sought refuge with Iroquoian-speaking Cayugas.

Even the direct linguistic evidence on which the Eastern Siouan classification is based is not as secure as one would wish. After a careful examination of the primary and secondary sources on three of Swanton's Virginia division "Eastern Siouans"—the Occaneechi, Saponi, and Tutelo—Carl F. Miller reached the conclusion that these groups were probably not Siouan speakers (1957:115-211). On the contrary, he found some evidence pointing to their speaking languages of the Algonquian stock. Although Miller's thesis is valuable in that it throws doubt into the "Eastern Siouan" theory, he goes too far, because the Tutelo language is definitely Siouan (Allen 1931:185-193; Voegelin 1941:246-249). In addition, his suggestion that the Siouan identity of the Catawba language be re-examined is hardly to the point. Siebert (1945) has established the Siouan identity of Catawba with relative certainty, although it does have certain grammatical peculiarities (Binford 1959; Sturtevant 1958).

However, even though the classification of Catawba as a

Siouan language is relatively certain, this does not take us far in understanding the broad outlines of Catawba prehistory. In fact, if the Siouan identity of Catawba leads us to think of them as "Eastern Siouans," in the sense meant by Mooney, it can be positively misleading. As a general rule, it is hazardous to extrapolate from linguistic classifications; with rare exceptions, one cannot expect to find a simple coincidence of linguistic, cultural, and racial boundaries. Indeed, the picture is already so confused we would do well to simply abandon the "Eastern Siouan" classification, admit that the hiatus in our knowledge of the Southeast still exists, and begin anew. As a point of departure, we can consider A. L. Kroeber's culture areas.

Kroeber locates the ancestors of the Catawbas in his South Atlantic Slope area, an area that includes most of South Carolina, North Carolina, and Virginia (Kroeber 1939:94). The northern border of the South Atlantic Slope area touches that of the Middle Atlantic Slope area inhabited by Algonquian-speakers and that of the Lower Great Lake area inhabited by the Iroquoian League and allied groups. To the west the South Atlantic Slope area is bounded by the Ohio Valley area, the latter being inhabited by the Illinois, Miami, and Shawnee, and by the Appalachian Summit area, the home of the Cherokees. To the South, near the Savannah River, Kroeber wisely draws a dotted line, a "doubtful" boundary between the South Atlantic Slope area and the Southeastern area, the territory of the historic Creek Indians (1939:Map No. 6).

Kroeber divides his South Atlantic Slope area into four subareas. The ancestors of the Catawbas were concentrated in the Piedmont subarea. This subarea, the largest of the four, embraces the central part of the piedmont physiographic area. It includes the territory between the Appalachian mountains and the fall-line of the rivers, except where this territory tapers into a thin triangle in northern Virginia and where it broadens into the hills of northern Georgia.[3] East of the fall-

---

3. The fall-line is an imaginary line drawn through the rapids of the rivers, marking the zone of transition between the hilly upper country and the flat low country. The fall-line lies close to the cities of Trenton, N. J., Richmond, Va., Halifax, N. C., Columbia, S. C., and Augusta, Ga.

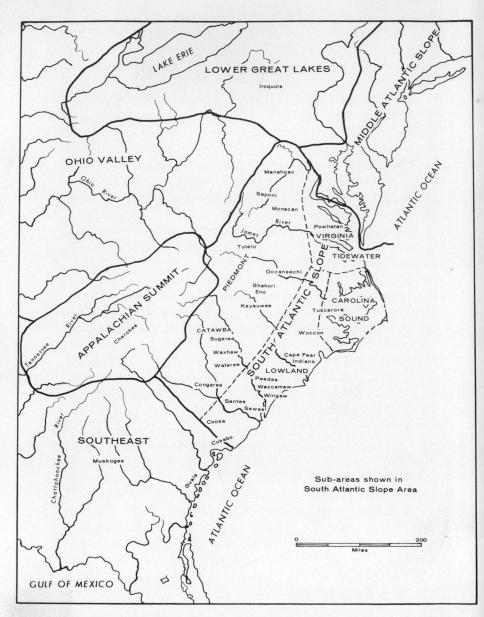

MAP 2. CULTURE AREAS OF THE EASTERN UNITED STATES,
SHOWING SELECTED NOMINATE INDIAN GROUPS, c. 1650.
Compiled from Kroeber and Swanton.

line, in the Atlantic coastal plain physiographic area, Kroeber distinguishes three subareas. The Virginia Tidewater subarea, bounded on the north by the Potomac River and on the south by the Dismal Swamp, was inhabited by the Powhatan Confederacy. South of this, separated by a "doubtful" boundary, lies the Carolina Sound subarea: it includes the territory inhabited by the Tuscarora and by other lesser known Iroquoian- and Algonquian-speaking peoples. South of the Carolina Sound subarea, running almost to the Savannah River, lies the Lowland subarea, by far the most indefinite and problematical of the four (cf. Binford 1967).

From the time of earliest European colonization the history of the southeastern United States has been profoundly influenced by a tripartite geographical division: these divisions are the mountains, the piedmont or "back country," and the "low country" bordering the coast. Although we must be wary of projecting the geography and ecology of one historical period back to an earlier period, there is considerable evidence that these divisions were also important in shaping the life of the aboriginal inhabitants. John Lederer, drawing on experience gained from three expeditions he claims to have made into the piedmont in 1669-70, reports that some Indians explicitly recognized these divisions. The mountains, or *Poemotinck*, were thought to be barren, inhabited only by cave-dwelling bears. The low country, or *Ahkynt*, embraced the area from the falls of the rivers to the coast. In between the mountains and the falls of the rivers lay the piedmont highlands, or *Akontshuck*. According to Lederer, the piedmont was inhabited by several "nations" speaking dialects of the same language (Lederer 1912).

Both Mooney and Swanton thought that the "Eastern Siouans" migrated into the piedmont area in relatively recent times, but subsequent archaeological research has revealed no evidence of such a migration. The societies that were present in the piedmont at the time of European colonization were not recent migrants; they were the products of several centuries of *in situ* social and cultural development.

Disregarding minor variations, the historic Indian groups of the piedmont were products of two major sources of social and cultural development. The central piedmont—

roughly limited by the northern and southern boundaries of
North Carolina—was populated by a number of Indian
groups whom Joffre Coe (1952) calls "hill tribes," a term
which avoids the linguistic implications of Mooney and
Swanton's "Eastern Siouans." These hill tribes were small
in population, but they shared a distinctive culture that was
similar in many ways to cultures situated north of them (cf.
Binford 1967:141). In the southern piedmont—mainly in
South Carolina—the hill tribes were in contact with people
who were culturally and socially quite different. These were
the southern chiefdoms, whose cultural affiliations were
with other cultures further south and west.[4] The southern
chiefdoms were more populous than the hill tribes, and
they had a more complex religious and political life; they were
the ancestors of the Creeks and Cherokees.

The physical and cultural ancestors of the hill tribes,
identified archaeologically as the Badin cultural complex,
first appeared in the piedmont around the beginning of the
Christian era (Coe 1964:121). Their pottery, tools, and
burial practices were similar to archaeological complexes to
the north; in addition, they were physically similar to the
Indian Knoll people of Kentucky (Coe 1952:306-307). From
the time of this entry until the early historic period the culture
of these hill tribes shows the influence of people to the north.
At the same time, they were remarkably conservative, even
insular. The archaeological record of the cultural development of the hill tribes shows remarkable conservatism and
resistance to change. For example, they never adopted the
Hopewell ceremonialism that became popular with their
neighbors (Coe 1952:307). Through several centuries of a
shifting hunting and gathering life, they gradually modified
their ceramic and lithic techniques and in time substituted
the bow and arrow for the atlatl and spear.

By around 1200 A.D. the hill tribes had incorporated agriculture into their economy. The resultant culture—identified
archaeologically as the Uwharrie cultural complex—was based
on an ecology in which hunting and gathering was an important pursuit, while the extra assurance of agriculture al-

---

4. My use of "tribe" and "chiefdom" accords with Elman R. Service's
formal definitions (1962:110-117).

lowed a more sedentary life. The cultivation of corn, beans, and squash enabled the hill tribes to settle down in villages. Subsequently, the Uwharrie culture became the most homogeneous and widespread culture in the development of the hill tribes; the slight variations from one location to another in previous times were absorbed into a single style. The greater stability and security afforded by agriculture is reflected in a minor population explosion. Uwharrie villages, clusters of small, circular houses made of saplings covered with skin and bark, were almost invariably situated on the banks of rivers (Lewis 1951:324). These villages gradually spread along the Yadkin River, northward towards Virginia, and southward toward the tributaries of the Santee River of South Carolina, the territory of the Catawba Indians of historic times (Coe 1952:307-308).

The southern chiefdoms were also the products of a long cultural development. Though cultural and linguistic differences existed among these chiefdoms, historical and archaeological research has turned up many basic similarities. They all made use of truncated pyramidal mounds, usually with ceremonial buildings on top. In association with the mound, they often laid out a plaza that was used for games and ceremonies. Power was centralized in the hands of political and religious functionaries (Griffin 1952:361-364). Their religious symbolism seems to have been similar, and this suggests that many of their beliefs must have been also.

Unlike among the conservative hill tribes, innovations seem to have spread rather rapidly among the southern chiefdoms. For example, in late prehistoric times a style of pottery called Lamar was developed. Apparently originating in central Georgia, it spread throughout Georgia, into South Carolina, and to a lesser extent, into Tennessee and eastern Alabama (Caldwell 1952:319). Thus, though there were linguistic and cultural differences among the pre-Creek and pre-Cherokee chiefdoms, the rapidity with which innovations spread suggests that there were many shared understandings.

The southern Appalachian mountains and foothills were almost certainly inhabited by the ancestors of the historic Cherokee Indians throughout the period in which we are interested. Although intensive archaeological research is just

beginning in this area, there is increasing evidence that the
ancestors of the Cherokee were occupying it toward the close
of the Archaic archaeological period, between 1,000 B.C.
and 0 A.D. (Coe 1961:57-60). Lounsbury's glottochronologi-
cal study shows that the Cherokee language split from the
Northern Iroquoian languages some 3,500 to 3,800 years ago
(1961:11-17). Contrary to traditional interpretations, it now
appears that the Cherokees were neither late migrants nor
homogeneous in their culture. Also contrary to traditional
interpretations is the certainty that the Cherokees adopted the
southeastern pyramidal mound complex with all that this
implies in terms of religious and social organization (Coe
1961:57-60). According to Mooney (1900), known historic
Cherokee settlements were situated south of the thirty-sixth
parallel (that is, south of what is now Knoxville, Tennessee).
The extent to which they ranged northward into the mountains and northeast into the piedmont can only be determined
by further archaeological research. It is entirely possible
that such research will provide a basis for Mooney's assertion
that the Cherokees once claimed the piedmont west of the
Catawba River. Although the prehistoric picture is not as
full as one would wish, it can safely be said that the Santee
River drainage area, the traditional territory of the Catawbas,
was a prehistoric meeting ground for the hill tribes and the
southern chiefdoms.

The boundaries of hill tribe territory are fairly clear
where they bordered the Cherokees and where they bordered
Iroquoian- and Algonquian-speaking peoples to the north
and northeast. The southeastern and eastern boundaries are
less clearly defined. From archaeological and historical sources
we know that pre-Creek chiefdoms were situated along the
Savannah River and along the southern coast of South Carolina. The precise extent to which the ancestors of the Creek
and Cherokee chiefdoms penetrated northward into the piedmont cannot be ascertained until further archaeological research is done in the Santee River drainage area and in the
low country south of the Peedee River.

South of the Tuscarora and the Carolina Sound Algonquians, the eastern boundary of the hill tribes is even more
obscure than the southeastern border. This is again partly due

to a lack of intensive archaeological research in lowland South and North Carolina. But even more, the eastern border has been obscured by an ethnohistorical error. Contrary to the argument presented here that the "Eastern Siouans" were hill tribes concentrated in the piedmont, Mooney includes in his Eastern Siouan classification the Indians of the Carolina lowlands from the Cape Fear River to the Santee River and its tributaries. This includes the Cape Fear, Waccamaw, Winyaw, Peedee, Sewee, Santee, Congaree, Wateree, and Waxhaw Indians (Mooney 1894:Pl. I).

An examination of the evidence on which this classification is based shows that it is inconclusive; if anything, the evidence suggests that the lowland Indians were culturally and linguistically different from the hill tribes. The presence of mounds along the lower Wateree and Peedee Rivers strongly suggests that the inhabitants were similar to the chiefdoms of coastal and inland Georgia (Lewis 1951:307-315; Caldwell 1952:320). From historical evidence alone, it is impossible to determine the linguistic and cultural affinities of the Winyaw, Waccamaw, and Cape Fear Indians; the latter are not even associated with an aboriginal name (Mooney 1894: 64-67, 76-77). Aside from their names, there is no evidence for the linguistic affinities of the Sewee, Peedee, Santee, Wateree, and Congaree. If the distinctive -ee ending is evidence for Siouan affiliation, as Swanton seems to have assumed, then the Yemasee, whom Swanton says were Muskogean-speakers, must also be counted as "Siouans" (Swanton 1922:80-109).

Lawson's observations on the lowland Indians do not indicate that they were culturally similar to the hill tribes. On the contrary, his description of the Waxhaws definitely suggests cultural affiliation with the southern chiefdoms; they practiced head deformation and other customs similar to a chiefdom which, as we shall presently see, moved up the Peedee River and into the piedmont in late prehistoric times. At the same time, Lawson's account clearly suggests that the Waxhaws were politically aligned with the Catawbas and the Saponi at the time of his visit.

Archaeological evidence indicates that in late prehistoric times the hill tribes in the southern piedmont were becoming culturally and socially similar to the chiefdoms which were ancestral to the Creeks and Cherokees. The archaeological record clearly shows that local cultural differences began to appear as the hill tribes reached their widest expansion. These changes began earliest and were most far-reaching in the southern part of the central piedmont—the area inhabited by the ancestors of the Catawbas. One dramatic change in the southern piedmont was the Lamar ceramic tradition. After being adopted by the ancestors of the Catawbas, this Lamar ceramic tradition spread to the northern piedmont area where it influenced the ceramics of the northern hill tribes. For example, it was adopted by the Sara Indians who were living on the Dan River around 1650, and by the Occaneechi Indians when they were living near the present Hillsboro, North Carolina. In addition, the Sara Indians were influenced to a lesser degree by the Fort Ancient people of the Ohio Valley (Coe 1952:308-311).

The insularity of the piedmont Indians ended with Spanish exploration in the sixteenth century. Between 1528 and 1567, exploratory expeditions were led by Panfilo de Narvaez, Hernando de Soto, Tristan de Luna, and Juan Pardo. Although these explorations were widely scattered and apparently involved little intimate contact, the Indians suffered heavy casualties, particularly from de Soto and Pardo. In 1569 the Spanish established a mission at Santa Elena, and they attempted to concentrate the Indians into permanent settlements in order to exploit them as food producers (Sturtevant 1962).

After the missions were established, the Spanish did not raid the coast and piedmont extensively for slaves. However, before this time slaving expeditions occasionally raided the coast. In 1521, for example, they raided the Indians living near Winyaw Bay and carried off about twenty people, one of whom—Francisco of Chicora—left the earliest lengthy description of a North American group (Swanton 1940:326). Apparently, these slave raids caused some of the Indians to move up the rivers to safety.

This possibly accounts for the movement of the Peedee culture, a southern chiefdom, into the upper Peedee River around 1550 A.D., where it remained for about a hundred years. The archaeological record of this intrusive Peedee culture is both dramatic and clear. The bearers of this culture were physically and culturally different from the hill tribes. While the hill tribes were narrow-headed, the Peedee people were round-headed and practiced head-deformation similar to the Waxhaw Indians observed by Lawson. They seem to have been more reliant on agriculture than the hill tribes, and they lived in larger villages. Unlike the hill tribes, they had square or rectangular public buildings, and they built pyramidal mounds, often with religious buildings on top.

As the Peedee culture became established, the hill tribes were apparently preempted from their home and forced to move up the Yadkin River and its tributaries. This pressure from outside may have forced the hill tribes to align with each other for mutual defense. Apparently, they did not borrow from the Peedee culture. After a century of occupation the Peedee people moved out, and the hill tribes reoccupied their recovered territory (Coe 1952:308-309).

Although much remains to be learned, we see that the ancestors of the Catawbas were situated where two cultural traditions met. The hill tribe culture pattern developed in the central piedmont, from whence it gradually spread north towards Virginia and south towards the Santee River drainage area. The picture is that of a number of small tribal groups, each tribe located in a village or several villages, exploiting their territory in accordance with a seasonal cycle of hunting, gathering, and agriculture. Since hunting was important, they probably guarded their hunting territory jealously, and if conflict occurred it was as likely to have been between cognate groups as with outsiders. The southern chiefdoms, which occupied the southern piedmont, had much the same ecology as did the hill tribes. However, the chiefdoms had more numerous populations and a more highly developed politico-religious life. In the Santee River drainage area, the territory of the ancestors of the Catawbas, these two cultural traditions met. Aside from this mixture, there are no indications of foreign intrusions in the piedmont until after the Spanish explorations in the sixteenth century (Coe 1964: 383-384).

As a physiographic area the piedmont is a narrow band

of hilly land bounded on the west by the Appalachian mountains and on the east by the Atlantic coastal plain. It begins in New York State, gradually widens as it runs through Pennsylvania, Maryland, and Virginia, becomes most expansive in the Carolinas, and terminates in northern Georgia and Alabama. The most characteristic features of the piedmont are its rolling hills, varying in elevation from 100 to 1,500 feet, and its rivers that rise in the mountains, cut swiftly through the piedmont to their rapids at the fall-line, and gradually become more sluggish and swampy in the coastal plain.

The piedmont physiographic area, being quite long from north to south, varies at these extremes in temperature and precipitation. Normal annual precipitation is 40 inches per year, except for the southern portion, where it is 50 to 60 inches per year. The normal annual temperature in the north is 50°F., while in the south it is 65°F. The most dramatic effect of these temperature variations is on the growth of plant life. In the southern piedmont, there are 50 or less days per year with little or no plant growth; in the central piedmont the time is 50 to 100 days; and in the northern piedmont there is little or no plant growth for 100 to 150 days per year. In the southern piedmont, corn, beans, and squash can safely be planted two to four weeks earlier than in the northern (Visher 1964:*passim*). This, of course, allowed for more intensive agricultural exploitation in the southern piedmont.

The Atlantic coastal plain physiographic area extends from the fall-line to the Atlantic coast; its terrain varies with nearness to the coast. Along the coast there are flat expanses of everglades and flatwoods where the soil is waterlogged for most of the year. Further inland the land is gently rolling but generally less than 100 feet above sea level. In general, the soil is poor because of inadequate drainage; it is decidedly swampy or marshy. The climate is somewhat warmer than in the piedmont, but average precipitation is about the same, varying from 40 to 55 inches per year.

Different topography and soils in the piedmont and coastal plain areas supported different flora and fauna. In the early colonial period, the piedmont was forested with deciduous trees, primarily oak, and a few pines. Some of these oak trees were so tall that Lawson could not kill the turkeys that perched in the tops of them, "though we shot very often, and our Guns were very good" (Lawson 1960:42). However, the piedmont was not thickly forested; on the contrary, there were great stretches of level, grassy country with widely separated trees. Consequently, travel on foot or horseback was easier in the piedmont than in the coastal plain.

The piedmont supported an abundance of large woodland game such as deer, bear, and elk. "They are always fat, I believe, with some delicate Herbage that grows on the Hills, for we find all Creatures that graze much fatter and better Meat on the Hills, than those in the Valleys: I mean towards and near the Sea" (Lawson 1960:127). Of these large game animals, the deer and bear were the most important in the Indian hunting economy. There were a few bison, but these were more a curiosity than a regular source of food and skins (Lawson 1960:119). The rivers were well stocked with fish, and in the spring there were large runs of herring and sturgeon swimming upriver to spawn. The piedmont people killed great quantities of sturgeon at the falls of the rivers; Indians living near the coast would not eat them for some reason. In addition, huge flocks of passenger pigeons roosted in the hills, particularly, it seems, at the headwaters of the Catawba and Yadkin Rivers.

I saw such prodigious Flocks of these Pigeons in January or February, 1701-2 (which were in the hilly Country between the great Nation of the Esaw-Indians and the pleasant Stream of Sapona, which is the West-Branch of Clarendon or the Cape Fair River) that they had broke down the Limbs of a great many large Trees all over those Woods whereon they chanced to sit and roost, especially the great Pines, which are a more brittle Wood than our sorts of Oak are (Lawson 1960:147-149).

As we shall presently see, these pigeons were an important source of food for the Catawba Indians.

In contrast to the predominantly deciduous cover of the piedmont, the Atlantic coastal plain was primarily covered by longleaf-loblolly pine, and while there was plenty of game it did not offer the variety and abundance of the piedmont. The main game animals were deer—though these were often thin—

and turkey. While traveling through the Atlantic coastal plain, Lawson and his party primarily relied on turkey for food. These were killed in large numbers, some weighing as much as forty pounds. Lawson's palate became so "Cloy'd with Turkey," that in desperation he ate an opossum, which he did not particularly relish because of its hairless, rat-like tail (Lawson 1960:3-4).

The villages and fields of the piedmont tribes and chiefdoms were regularly situated on the banks of rivers and creeks. In colonial accounts, the fields deserted by aboriginal agriculturalists are called "old fields." Virtually all of the piedmont old fields were situated on the banks of rivers. Edward Bland's description of agricultural fields along the Meherrin or Woodford River is a good example: "Immediately after the passage over this River, are old Indian fields of exceedingly rich land, that bears two crops of Indian corne a yeare. . . ." (1912:120). Batts and Fallam made similar observations on their expedition to the New River, a stream running north and west into the Kanawha River, a tributary of the Ohio River. "Due west, the soil, the farther we went (is) the richer and full of bare meadows and old fields" (Alvord 1912:189). In addition, there is some evidence that the Indians preferred the bottoms along the creeks and branches that were tributaries of the rivers. Here they avoided the devastation of swift river floods while retaining the advantage of annual sedimentary deposits.

The reasons for this "riverine agriculture" in river and creek bottoms are fairly clear. Away from the river bottoms the soil of the piedmont is subject to severe sheet and gully erosion. In the central piedmont this erosion is even greater than in the northern piedmont; in the north the freezing of the soil inhibits erosion during the winter months, while in the south erosion occurs all year (Visher 1954:356-357). Lawson says that the soil of Carolina is "vastly rich, especially on the Freshes of the Rivers, one part bearing great Timbers, others being Savannas or natural Meads, where no Trees grow for several Miles, adorned by Nature with a pleasant Verdure, and beautiful Flowers, frequent in no other places, yielding abundance of Herbage for Cattle, Sheep, and Horses" (Lawson 1960:80-81). Another factor is that this river bottom soil was "light" and easy to work with simple tools. Essentially, riverine agriculture consisted of multiple cropping (two or more crops in the same field in one year) and intercropping (several vegetables in the same field) on small but very fertile pieces of land (Murphy and Hudson 1968). It was quite different from slash-and-burn or swidden agriculture.

Drawing on both historical and archaeological data, the basic ecological pattern of the piedmont was that of year-round hunting and gathering with seasonal emphases on riverine agriculture and the procurement of certain kinds of game. The pattern of ecological activities followed a regular annual cycle. Throughout the year piedmont people engaged in casual hunting for small game, fishing for fresh-water fish, and gathering various fruits, berries, and roots. However, all of these activities were supplementary to the primary subsistence techniques.

The primary subsistence techniques varied with the season. In the summer two or three crops of corn and several varieties of beans, squash, and gourds were raised (Lawson 1960:76-78). Unlike the Iroquois, whose women did most of the agricultural work, piedmont agriculture seems to have been a man's pursuit. Some of the vegetables were eaten green, while the remainder were dried and preserved for the lean months. In the fall there was an emphasis on gathering forest products, particularly nuts. Lawson suggests that the Indians relied primarily on hickory nuts and chinkapins, the latter "a sort of Chestnut" (1960: 100-101). In winter when the woods were dry, the main pursuit was communal hunting of large woodland game, particularly deer. Their main technique was using fire surrounds which drove "the Deer and other Game into small Necks of Land and Isthmuses where they kill and destroy what they please" (1960:219-220). The men, accompanied by their wives, left their main villages and traveled several days away, leaving behind older people and children. The dominant pursuit in spring was catching the sturgeon and herring that swam up the rivers in great numbers to spawn. The Indians used weirs, snares, long poles with nets attached to the ends, and other devices to catch these fish.

This was the basic ecological pattern for the piedmont, and with modifications it probably held for much of the Southeast. Within this basic pattern, however, local resources often allowed for advantageous variations. The passenger pigeon, for example, allowed the Catawbas such a variation.

In some parts where Pigeons are plentiful, they get of their fat enough to supply their Winter Stores. Thus, they abide in these Quarters all the Winter long, till the Time approaches for planting their Maize and other Fruits. In these quarters, at Spare-hours, the Women make Baskets and Mats to lie upon, and those that are not extraordinary Hunters, make Bowls, Dishes and Spoons, of Gumwood, and the Tulip-Tree, others (where they find a Vein of White Clay, fit for their purpose) make Tobacco-pipes, all which are often transported to other Indians, that perhaps have greater Plenty of Deer and other Game; so they buy, with these Manufactures, their raw Skins, with the Hair on, which our neighboring Indians bring to their Towns, and in the Summertime, Make the Slaves and sorry Hunters dress them, the Winter-Sun being not strong enough to dry them; and those that are dried in the Cabins are black and nasty with the Light-Wood Smoke, which they commonly burn (Lawson 1960:220-221).

By exploiting the passenger pigeon as storable food, the Catawbas enjoyed considerable leisure during winter months. When the colonial fur trade began, the Catawbas were able to devote this leisure to the acquisition of hides. Consequently, they had a considerable economic advantage over people who had to hunt for food during the winter months.

If this interpretation of piedmont ecology is correct, then we need to re-examine Kroeber's explanation of low population in the eastern United States in terms of "insane, unending, continuously attritional" warfare (1939:148). While warfare or raiding was definitely important in the Southeast, early colonial references to continual Indian wars were often rationalizations for enslaving the Indians, the argument being that they were better off as slaves than tortured to death by the Indians who were their enemies (Crane 1959:114, 139). Ironically, we shall presently see that in early colonial times most of this Indian "warfare" was stimulated by Charleston traders as a means of acquiring slaves.

The low population density of the piedmont has led to

its being regarded as something of a cultural sink-hole, an area marginal to the more highly developed cultures surrounding it (Coe 1952:301). The tenacity of this view has led some anthropologists—notably those who follow Mooney—to the wholly unwarranted conclusion that the people of the piedmont almost exclusively relied on a hunting and gathering ecology (Mooney 1894:9). As we have seen, neither archaeological nor historical data bear this out. Before the Spanish came, the central piedmont witnessed the development of an ecological pattern that combined hunting and gathering with riverine agriculture. Though emphases may have differed, this seems to have been the ecological pattern for most of the Southeast.

Yet there is some truth in the view that the central piedmont was less developed than surrounding areas. That is, it may be that the hill tribes were not as highly organized as their ecological pattern would permit. Historical evidence clearly indicates that the Cherokees of the Appalachian mountains and foothills, the Virginia Tidewater Algonquians, and the Muskogean-speaking peoples of inland Georgia were organized into relatively complex chiefdoms. For these societies there is ample evidence of a moderately dense population, office-holding chiefs, centers for politico-religious activities, elements of hierarchical organization, and redistributive economics (Swanton 1946:619-782). Furthermore, Fred Gearing (1962) has argued that the Cherokee developed a form of state organization in the middle of the eighteenth century.

Although the evidence is fragmentary, the historic societies along the Georgia coast and the South Carolina coast south of the Santee River seem also to have been chiefdoms. At the time Charleston was founded, the Cusabo was a loose confederacy located between the Savannah and Edisto Rivers; it may even have extended to the Santee River to include the Santee, Sewee, and other groups (Milling 1940:35-50). However, caution is necessary here because the Cusabo confederacy, as well as the Powhatan confederacy in Virginia, could have been stimulated by Spanish contact.

While information on the social organization of the hill tribes is meager, there are definite suggestions that they were not as centrally organized as the chiefdoms surrounding them.

Several things lead one to believe that the hill tribes were neither very populous nor very responsive to hierarchical organization. For one thing, the hill tribes were never as important to the South Carolina colonists as were the Creeks and Cherokees, both of whom played the role of allies, enemies, and traders in skins and slaves (Crane 1959:132, 179-180). While the English were often able to mobilize as many as a thousand Creek Indians for punitive and slaving expeditions, Colonel John Barnwell had little success in mobilizing the hill tribes against the Tuscarora in 1711-12. Starting with two companies of piedmont people recruited in the Carolinas, only a handful remained when Barnwell reached the heart of Tuscarora country (Milling 1940:118-121).

The Indians in Lawson's account are generally egalitarian, though this must be taken with the proviso that it is not always clear whether he is generalizing about the hill tribes, Tuscarora, or coastal Algonquians: "Their Tongue allows not to say, *Sir, I am your Servant;* because they have no different Titles for Man, only King, War-Captain, Old Man, or Young, which respect the Stations and Circumstances Men are employed in, and arrived to, and not Ceremony." In other words, they had words for statuses but not for positions in a prestige hierarchy. They had "slaves," but these were different from slaves in the usual sense.

As for Servants, they have no such thing, except Slave, and their Dogs, Cats, tame or domestic Beasts, and Birds, are called by the same name. For the Indian Word for Slaves includes them all. So when an Indian tells you he has got a Slave for you, it may (in general Terms, as they use) be a young Eagle, a Dog, Otter or any other thing of Nature, which is obsequiously to depend on the Master for Sustenance (Lawson 1960:213).

In many cases, these slaves were probably displaced persons from Indian societies decimated by disease and war.

The hill tribe "King" seems to have been a headman, at least some of whom came into their office by matrilineal succession. He did not have coercive powers; decisions were reached through the deliberation of the "King," his "War-Captains," and "Counsellors" or elders. "After every Man has given his Opinion, that which has most Voices, or, in Summing up, is found to be most reasonable, that they make use of without any Jars and Wrangling, and put in Execution, the first Opportunity that offers" (Lawson 1960:207-208).

Significantly, perhaps, the King of the Santees was an exception, supposedly having the power to put any of his people to death who were guilty of a crime which he thought merited execution. Among other groups, Lawson says that the usual reaction to murder was blood revenge by a kinsman of the murdered person, or by compensation (Lawson 1960:207). However, the Santee were both in direct contact with Charleston traders and much reduced by disease. There is also a suggestion of nativism: in the company of the Santee King, Lawson met a "Priest" or "Conjurer" who had the promise of "the white Man above" to make his people "equal with the white People in making Guns, Ammunitions, &c" (Lawson 1960:13-16). Thus, the power of the Santee King could indicate chiefly organization, or it could reflect nativistic charisma.

There is nothing in Lawson's account of the hill tribes suggesting redistributive economics similar to that of the Creeks (Bartram n.d.:401). When a man's home was destroyed by fire, the people assembled, and "Speakers, or grave old Men" made speeches about the virtues of reciprocity. "After this Oration is over, every Man, according to his Quality, throws him down upon the Ground some Present, which is commonly Beads, Ronoak, Peak, Skins, or Furs, and which very often amounts to treble the Loss he has suffered." When a woman with children was widowed, they made "their young men plant, reap, and do everything that she is not capable of doing herself" (Lawson 1960:188-189). While successful warriors and hunters had great prestige, Lawson says that the Indians did not envy those who had wealth.

Several of the Indians are possessed of a great many Skins, Wampums, Ammunition, and what other things are esteemed amongst them; yet such an Indian is no more esteemed amongst them, than any other ordinary fellow, provided he has no personal Endowments which are the Ornaments that must gain him an Esteem among them; for a great Dealer amongst the Indians, is not otherwise respected and esteemed than as a Man that Strains his Wits and fatigues himself to furnish others with

Necessaries of Life that live much lower and enjoy more of the world than he himself does with all his Pelf (1960:208-209).

Although Lawson says they were not envious in the manner of Europeans, there are indications that both envy and hatred were present, though suppressed by an ideology of kinship amity.

Contrary to Mooney's and Swanton's interpretation, the bulk of the evidence indicates that the Catawbas of the late seventeenth century were culturally affiliated with the southern chiefdoms, forming some kind of confederacy. As Lawson journeyed up the Catawba River he successively passed through the territory of the Waxhaws, Esaws, Sugerees, and Catawbas, the latter being furthest north and nearest to the Cherokees. Unlike the hill tribes, all of these groups were populous. In every village, beginning with the Waxhaws, Lawson saw a "town-house" similar to those Bartram observed among both the Creeks and the Cherokees (n.d.:357).

Lawson says that the last town house he saw was at Saponi, situated northeast of the Catawbas on the upper Peedee River. However, since this is in the territory vacated by the Peedee Culture about fifty years before Lawson's journey, it is possible that the Saponi were a hill tribe merely occupying a deserted Peedee village. Hill tribe re-occupation of deserted Peedee sites has been archaeologically verified (Coe 1952:308). At Saponi, Lawson first mentions seeing protective palisades that were common in the northern piedmont. At the time of Lawson's visit, the Saponi were considering confederation with two other hill tribes, the Tutelo and the Keyauwee. The three, being small, "were going to live together, by which they thought they should strengthen themselves and become formidable to their Enemies" (1960:43-47).

Lawson made other observations suggesting that the Catawbas and their confederates shared culture traits with both the Cherokees and Muskogeans. The most outstanding Muskogean trait appears in the detailed description of Waxhaw head deformation. He does not specifically mention this practice for the Esaw, Sugeree, or Catawba. In speaking of the Waxhaws, he says: "These Indians are of an extraordinary Stature, and *called by their Neighbors* flat Heads, which seems a very suitable Name for them" (1960:30, italics mine). This phraseology suggests that head deformation was used only by the Waxhaws. Head deformation is known to have been used by the Natchez, Taensa, Tunica, Houma, Chitimacha, Caddo, Choctaw, and Chickasaw (Swanton 1946: 540-541). There is no historical evidence of head deformation among the (historic) Creeks, Cherokee, Quapaw, Shawnee, hill tribes, or the Algonquians of North Carolina and Virginia, although we know from archaeological evidence that the ancestors of the Creeks and Cherokees practiced it. Later on the Catawbas were sometimes called "Flat Heads," but this usage was generally limited to the Iroquois who referred to the entire Catawba confederacy by this designation.

In other respects the Waxhaws resemble the Cherokees. The dance that Lawson (1960:34-36) witnessed in the Waxhaw town-house is remarkably similar to a dance Bartram (n.d.: 297-300) witnessed at Cowee, a Cherokee town. The similarities are: (1) preliminary oratory, (2) dancing girls, (3) costumed male dancers, and (4) sexual license. The similarity extends even to the way in which the fire in the town-house was made of small pieces of wood or cane; this fuel was arranged in a circle such that it could be continuously replenished while the fire burned around it.[5]

It is even possible to argue that the word "Catawba" suggests Cherokee cultural affinities. Speck was never able to satisfactorily explain the origin or etymology of "Catawba."

The proper name Catawba with its derivatives has been in general use among colonial writers for two centuries and forms the basis of the names by which the tribe is known among other Indian groups of the east, yet no satisfactory explanation of its origin or etymology can be offered. To the speakers of the language it is a proper name with a fixed designation but having no interpretation of which they are conscious (Speck 1939:407-408).

Yet, Mooney noted the similarity between "Catawba" and Cherokee "*kituhwa*," an ancient settlement of Cherokees

---

5. The pieces of wood or cane were criss-crossed, suggesting the scales of a serpent; the fire moved in a circular path, suggesting the movement of the sun. Both the sun and the serpent are important in southeastern symbolism (Mooney 1900:230).

on the Tuckasegee River, near the present Bryson City,
North Carolina (Mooney 1900:182). These people were
the northernmost Cherokees. Perhaps for this reason, the
Delawares, Shawnees, and other northern Algonquians collectively referred to the Cherokees as "Cuttawa," "Gattoch-
wa," "Kittuwa," and so forth (Mooney 1900:15, 182).

Mooney, Swanton, and Speck could not accept this
derivation of "Catawba" because they made several misleading
assumptions. (1) They assumed that the Cherokees were
relatively recent invaders. As we have seen, subsequent
archaeological research shows that this is false. (2) They
assumed that the Cherokees at the beginning of the eighteenth
century were internally harmonious. As Gearing points
out, this was not so. In the early eighteenth century, the
Cherokees were an aggregate of politically independent villages (1962:5). (3) They assumed that the Catawbas of the
early eighteenth century spoke a Siouan language. This is
not necessarily true. After 1800 the Catawbas are known to
have spoken a Siouan language, as all the vocabularies collected after that show. But in 1743 the "Catawbas" included
people speaking over *twenty* different dialects and languages,
some of which were definitely non-Siouan (Adair 1930:235-
236). What assurance do we have that the standard Catawba
"court dialect" spoken at that time is ancestral to the language
spoken after 1800? That is, the language we know as Catawba
could just as easily be descended from one of the nineteen
other dialects spoken.

The conclusion is inescapable that the Catawbas of the
early eighteenth century were *culturally* affiliated with the
Cherokees. It is even possible that some of them may have
spoken a dialect of Cherokee, and this is perfectly compatible
with the fact that others among them spoke a Siouan
language.

One further point must be mentioned. Until about 1710
the Indians living on the Catawba River were collectively
called "Esaws." After this they were collectively referred to
as "Catawbas." In the pages that follow, I will generally use
"Cawtaba" in this collective sense, referring to Indians who
were culturally heterogeneous, but who represented a socially
meaningful category.

Chapter III

The Catawba Nation as a Colonial Satellite

THE history of the Catawba Indians, like that of all people who trace descent from preliterate ancestors, grows increasingly dim as it recedes into the past. The Catawba Indians and their neighbors are among the most poorly documented aboriginal people in North America (Mooney 1894:6). In part this is because they, along with the Iroquoian- and Algonquian-speaking Indians of the Atlantic coast, lay directly in the path of English traders and small-scale agriculturists. Furthermore, the English were worse ethnographers than either the French or the Spanish. They neither had the missionary interests of the Spanish nor the French proclivity for working within the framework of aboriginal politics. Even the seventeenth and eighteenth century Virginia traders, who by virtue of their long periods of residence among the piedmont Indians knew them most intimately, left only scraps of information that are more tantalizing than informative. Consequently, primary historical material on the early Catawbas and their neighbors is largely limited to a few accounts by explorers and the records of colonial governments.

At the close of the seventeenth century the Catawbas were a confederacy with socially and culturally affiliated chiefdoms like the Waxhaw and Sugeree, and they were in communication with hill tribes like the Saponi. Historical sources do not reveal how long the Catawba confederacy had been in existence at the time of Lawson's visit in 1701, but it is likely that it was then only a few decades old. From Lawson's observations, it is clear that the Catawbas occupied the position of middlemen in the Virginia trade. Lawson, for

example, met a man named John Stewart, a Virginia trader
residing with the Catawba King, "who had traded there for
many Years" (Lawson 1960:40-41).

Specialization in trade is further indicated by the Catawba
King having two or three "trading girls" in his cabin.

They set apart the youngest and prettiest Faces for Trading
Girls; these are remarkable by their Hair, having a particular
Tonsure by which they are known and distinguished from those
engaged to Husbands. They are mercenary, and whoever makes
Use of them, first hires them, the greatest Share of the Gain
going to the King's Purse, who is the chief Bawd, exercising his
Perogative over all the Stews of his Nation, and his own Cabin
(very often,) being the chiefest Brothel-House (Lawson 1960:
32).

One of Lawson's companions hired the services of one of
these trading girls. During the night while he was asleep, she
picked his pockets and stole his shoes as well. The next
morning Lawson dryly observed "our Spark already repent
his new Bargain, walking barefoot in his Penetentials, like
some poor Pilgrim to Loretto."

Several statements by Stewart show that the Catawbas
had an extensive communication network. He had heard
that Lawson's party was coming about twenty days before
their arrival. This would have been about the time Lawson
made contact with the Santee Indians above the French plantations on the Santee River. Stewart had also heard that
"Sinnagers" (Iroquois) were abroad in Virginia. Thus the
Catawbas were informed of events occurring 125 to 175 miles
away.

The unmistakable dominance of the Catawbas in 1700
was a function of their having an advantageous relationship
with Virginia traders. The history of the piedmont in the
late seventeenth and early eighteenth century was powerfully
shaped by the Virginia traders. Somewhat later it was even
more powerfully affected by the traders from Charleston.

Verner Crane has argued that the relationships between
Europeans and Indians, including the Indian wars, were quite
different in the southern and northern colonies (1959:162).
The early history of the north is dominated by the competition for land between small-scale colonial agriculturalists

and Indians; early southern history, on the other hand, is dominated by conflicts stimulated by Charleston fur traders. Crane's argument also applies to the piedmont, although the first agents of conflict were traders from Virginia, whose trade assumed only a fraction of the importance in the Virginia economy that it had in the South Carolina economy.

Although Virginians were interested in exploring and exploiting the piedmont early in the seventeenth century, serious exploration and trade did not begin until after Opechancanough's massacre of 1644 (Alvord and Bigood 1912-28-29).[1] Beginning in 1645, a series of forts were built at the falls of the James, Appomattox, Pamunkey, Rappahannock, Blackwater, and Nansemond Rivers; subsequently these forts became points of departure for exploration and trade. Using capital gained through economic concessions, the commanders of these forts organized and financed the trade to the piedmont Indians. The most successful of these traders was Abraham Wood, the commander of Fort Henry at the falls of the Appomattox River, near the site of present day Petersburg, Virginia. From this strategic location the Occaneechi trading path ran the length of the piedmont to the Catawbas and to the Lower Cherokees; another trading path went from Fort Henry to the Kanawha River and to yet another route to the Cherokees (Meyer 1928:Plate 15).[2]

The traders who set out from Fort Henry were Wood's servants and employees, or private traders who received their goods on credit and contracted to pay a stipulated price when they returned. For transportation they used pack horses, each of which carried about 150 to 200 pounds of goods. In the piedmont it was possible to travel on horseback about twenty miles a day (Alvord and Bigood 1912:33).

It is difficult to determine when this trade assumed a significant volume. The account by Edward Bland of a

1. Soon after the founding of Jamestown in 1607, the Virginians conducted a trade to tidewater Virginia, Chesapeake Bay, and to Indians somewhat farther north. By the middle of the seventeenth century, this trade had become insignificant in volume (Neil 1932:3).

2. The Occaneechi trading path first went to Occaneechi Island on the Roanoke River. In the closing decades of the seventeenth century, when it was extended south to Catawba and Cherokee territory, it was called "the Catawba trading path" (Neil 1932:7).

trip to the falls of the Roanoke River in 1650, in the company
of Abraham Wood, indicates that Virginia traders had already been in the area (Bland 1912:109-130). However,
their trade was apparently low in volume because few of the
Indians had firearms, this being a rough index of extensive
trade. For example, prompted by curiosity, the "Maharineck
great men" asked members of the Bland and Wood expedition
to fire their guns; when they complied, some of the people
in the village fled to the woods in fear. However, when a
different group of Indians subsequently reported to Bland
and Wood that they had heard a gun go off, their "Ap-
pamattuck" guide surmised that it had been fired by
"Wainoake Spies."

Even though Virginia law prohibited the sale of arms and
ammunition to Indians, in 1670 John Lederer and his companions were welcomed into a Monacan village by volleys
of shot fired in the air as greetings (Lederer 1912:149). In
addition, it is clear from Lederer's account that the Susquehanna had firearms. Lederer advises traders to fire their
guns as a signal before entering the villages of Indians with
whom the Susquehanna were friendly; but for those with
whom the Susquehanna were not friendly, Lederer says it
would "affright and dispose them to some treacherous practice" because they were not familiar with firearms (Lederer
1912:169). In 1671 Batts and Fallam found firearms in the
Saponi village then situated on the Staunton River. "Here
we were very joyfully and kindly received with firing of
guns and plenty of provisions" (Fallam 1912:185). Also,
while in the Tutelo village then located near present day
Salem, Virginia, they gave "three or four shots of powder" to
a Mohetan Indian whose people were then living on the
Kanawha River (Fallam 1912:193).

Thus by 1671 trade appears to have been fairly extensive
among the northern hill tribes, as evidenced by the fact that
most of them had firearms. The usual practice of traders was
first to trade trinkets and small cutlery; later they traded larger
tools, arms, and ammunition. While this trade was expanding
in the north, the Westo, a small group living on the Savannah
River, were using firearms to inflict heavy casualties among

the coastal Indians.[3] Since Spanish policy strictly forbade trading firearms to these coastal Indians, the contest was unequal (Sturtevant 1962:67). Crane infers that Virginia must have been the source of these firearms and that the Westo must have come from the north. This is plausible, but it can just as easily be explained another way. Abraham Wood, for example, reports that the southern Appalachian "Tomahittans" who visited him in 1673 had about sixty guns which were not of English manufacture; they were almost certainly Spanish (Wood 1912:214). Wood goes on to repeat information given by Gabriel Arthur, one of his employees who lived with the Tomahittans in order to learn their language. Undoubtedly this was a preliminary to trade. They forced Arthur to accompany them on several raids, and in his account of these raids the method by which they acquired the guns is clear. On one raid, after waiting in ambush for seven days on the outskirts of a Spanish settlement, they saw "a Spanniard with a gentille habitt, accoutered with gunn, sword and pistoll. one [sic] of ye Tomahittans espieing him att a distance crept up to ye path side and shot him to death" (Wood 1912:219).[4]

It is unlikely that the Virginia traders were in direct contact with the Catawbas and their confederates before 1680, and it is doubtful that guns were generally available more than a decade before Lawson's visit.[5] As late as 1701, it is clear from Lawson's account that the "Wateree Chickanee"

---

3. The identity of the Westo is a matter of dispute. Swanton generally argued that they were a band of Yuchi, while Crane argued that they were not Yuchi, and that they came from the north. In a recent review of this controversy, Carol Irwin Mason argues that Swanton's Westo-Yuchi identification is inconclusive, and that the Westo were more likely to have been Iroquoian, Algonquian, or Siouan-speaking people from the north (Mason 1963:1342-1346). If the Westo were the same as the "Ricohockans" who attacked European settlements in Virginia in 1656, as Mason states, then they could well have been Cherokee, since Mooney lists "Ricohockan" in his Cherokee synonymy (1900:183-184).

4. Swanton felt that the "Tomohittans" were the same as the Westo, arguing that both were Yuchi (1922:183-191). However, it is rather more likely that they were Cherokees. "Tomahittan" could be derived from "Tomasee," "Tennessee," etc.—Cherokee place names.

5. A trader named Cadwallader Jones is said to have traded 400 miles SSW from his fort on the Rappahannock River in Virginia in 1681. However, he was apparently trading peake and roanoke for skins (Harrison 1922:327).

were less well supplied than the Waxhaw to the north and
the Congaree to their south, the former trading directly with
Virginians and the latter with South Carolinians (Lawson
1960:28-29).

The Virginia trade to the piedmont, unlike the Charleston
trade to the southern Indians, was primarily a commercial ven-
ture. The Charleston trader like his Virginia counterpart was
primarily interested in profit, but his trade was regulated
(with mixed success) by a government that was interested in
arming Indians to secure their allegiance against the French,
the Spanish, and their Indian allies. The Virginians used trade
as a means of gaining Indian allies for only a brief period of
time (Binford 1967:163-185). These differences aside, the
Virginia traders, particularly those who lived with the Indians
for long periods of time, gained considerable power in piedmont politics. Abraham Wood, for example, tells us that James
Needham, one of his employees, was allowed to pass through
the Occaneechi village on his way to the Tomahittans only
through the intercession of a man named Henry Hatcher,
an independent trader who was then residing with the Occaneechi (Wood 1912:215).

The power in the hands of the Virginia traders produced
two interrelated effects in the political systems of the piedmont Indians. First, through his monopoly of trade goods the
trader could bestow his favor on any Indian or group of
Indians he chose; consequently he could reinforce the internal power structure of a tribe in any way he chose. In
the interest of profit the traders rewarded those who provided the most skins, whether they gained them as hunters
or as entrepreneurs. Through this power, the traders were
able to reinforce indigenous power structures along different
lines and modify their character. In spite of what Lawson says
about Indians' lack of envy, these traders must have caused
considerable conflict within the Indian societies. Second,
because trade goods were a source of wealth and power,
neighboring Indian societies competed with each other in
becoming middlemen in the trade, thus exercising some control over it.

The precise nature of the first of these effects escapes us
because the Virginia traders left little or no account of

their dealings with Indians. Their failure in this was intentional; disclosure of their knowledge would have been an advantage to their competition. In addition, they wanted to conceal their illegal trade in arms and ammunition. During the Yamassee War, for example, the South Carolinians accused the Virginia traders of selling arms and ammunition to the Indians who almost succeeded in wiping them out (Crane 1959:176-177).

The second effect of the Virginia traders on the piedmont Indians is more satisfactorily documented. The Indians who had the best access to trade had a military and commercial advantage over less fortunate Indians. Like the Iroquois in the northern colonies, the piedmont Indians and the Indians bordering the piedmont attempted to become middlemen. The "Wainoakes" attempted this at an early date, and the divisive effects of their attempt can be seen in Edward Bland's account of the 1650 expedition. While in a Meherrin village Bland met a visiting Tuscarora Indian who said that his people wanted to visit the Virginia settlements for trade, but they were discouraged from doing so by the "Wainoakes" who told them "that the English would kill them or detaine them, and would not let them goe without a great heape of Roanoke middle high." Bland then told the Tuscarora that the Wainoakes "had likewise spoken much against the Tuskarood [sic] to the English, it being a common thing amongst them to villifie one another, and tell nothing but lies to the English" (Bland 1912:119).

Later, perhaps after the "Wainoakes" were expelled, the Tuscarora attempted to control some of the trade to the piedmont. For example, after Lawson and his party swung south of the Occaneechi village near present day Hillsboro, North Carolina, they encountered two Tuscarora Indians who told them that the English were a wicked people who would not allow the Indians to hunt. They succeeded in dissuading two of Lawson's Indian companions from going any further. Lawson adds, "These two fellows were going among the Shoccores and Achonechy Indians to sell their Wooden Bowls and Ladles for Raw Skins, which they make great Advantage of, hating that any of these westward Indians should have any Commerce with the English which would prove a Hinderance to their

Gains" (1960:57). In addition, the Tuscarora carried rum several hundred miles to trade with piedmont Indians. These Tuscarora traders refused to conduct business in any language but their own, "therefore their Tongue is understood by some in every Town of all the Indians near us." Lawson further says that this was true of other "powerful Nations" trading with others "of fewer Numbers and less Power" (Lawson 1960:239).

The Occaneechi made an early attempt to establish themselves on the trade route and to dominate other Indians by controlling the trade to the southern piedmont. We have already seen that James Needham needed the intercession of Henry Hatcher before he could proceed south to meet Gabriel Arthur and the Tomahittans. When Hatcher reported this to Abraham Wood, he also reported that an Occaneechi Indian named "Indian John" or "Hasecoll" later murdered Needham in the vicinity of the Yadkin River while they were *en route* to the Tomahittans (Wood 1912:217-218). Undoubtedly this murder was motivated by the Occaneechi's interest in protecting their trade to the south (Rothrock 1929:5).

In 1674, when Arthur was returning to Fort Henry in the company of several Tomahittans carrying packs of trade goods, they found four Occaneechis waiting in the Sara village. When these Occaneechis attempted to murder Arthur during the night, he managed to get away and hide. Failing in their attempt, the Occaneechis returned to their own village, and the Tomahittans fled for their lives, leaving their packs behind. The next morning Arthur returned to the Sara village and hired four Sara Indians to carry the packs deserted by the Tomahittans. They accompanied him to Eno, but beyond this neither the Sara nor the Eno would "goe forth with his packs for feare of ye Occenechees" (Wood 1912:223-224).

Arthur left the packs with the Eno, passed through the Occaneechi territory under cover of darkness, and returned to Fort Henry, where about a month later he met the "king of ye Tomahittans," his two sons, and one other companion. After the attempted murder at Sara, they had circumvented the Occaneechi by going north through the Tutelo village at the headwaters of the Staunton River; from there they went to the James River, built a "canoe of barke," and descended to the Monacan village. They then proceeded on foot to Fort Henry. Wood sums it up in this way:

Hee (the Tomahittan "king") staid with me a few dayes promising to bee with mee againe att ye fall of ye leafe with a party that would not be frited by ye way and doubt not but hee will come if hee bee not intercepted by selfe ended traders for they have strove what they could to block up ye designe from ye beginning. Which (sic) were here too tedious to relate. Thus endes ye tragedy I hope yett to live to write cominically of ye business. If I could have ye countenance of some person of honour in England to curb and bridle ye obstructers here for here there is no incouragement att all to be had. . . .

It is clear from Wood's account that the Occaneechi owed their existence to trade. They were as interested in blocking trade as the Tomahittans (Cherokees) were in securing it. It also seems that the Occaneechi were a composite group: ". . . they are but a handful of people, besides what vaga-bonds repair to them it beeing a receptakle for rogues" (Wood 1912: 225-226).

In 1676 the Occaneechi successfully withstood an attack by 200 Virginians led by Nathaniel Bacon, but in doing so they reportedly lost 50 men (Mooney 1894:54-55; Neil 1932: 7). Some time between this date and 1701 they moved to a site near the present Hillsboro, North Carolina, where Law-son found them on his trip (Lawson 1960:53-54). Later they moved to Fort Christanna, Virginia, along with the Saponi, Tutelo, and others (Mooney 1894:55).

The history of the Occaneechi parallels that of the Catawbas. In 1700 the Catawba confederacy owed its emi-nence to position of middleman in the Virginia trade. As we have seen, there are indications that the Cherokees were anxious to acquire European goods in the late seventeenth century. However, because the Charleston traders first took their goods to the Muskogean-speaking Indians, bypassing the Cherokees, they received few goods from Charleston until after 1717 (Neil 1932:9, 13-14). Furthermore, the Virginia traders never succeeded in finding a satisfactory northern route to the Cherokees. Writing in 1728, William Byrd complains about the exhausting route through Catawba territory, wishing for "a shorter cut to carry on so profitable a Trade" (Byrd 1929:246).

Eventually the Virginia traders went through Catawba territory and made direct contact with the Cherokees (Neil 1932:17), but at first they unloaded their goods and exchanged them for skins in Catawba territory. From here, some of the Catawbas carried the goods south to trade with Indians in the Carolina back country. Lawson, for example, met a "War-Captain" who was on his way to trade with "Congarees and Savannas." "He had a Man-Slave with him who was loaded with European Goods, his Wife and Daughter being in Company" (1960:39-40).

Some of the Catawbas must have conducted a similar trade with the Cherokees to their northwest. The supposed perpetual enmity between the Cherokees and the "Eastern Siouans" has been greatly exaggerated. More precisely, there was enmity between Cherokees and Catawbas after the middle of the eighteenth century, but it is a mistake to project this back to the beginning of the century. For example, when the English in 1715 attempted to persuade the Conjurer, a Cherokee leader, to align his Lower Towns with the English in the Yamassee War, he tried to clear the Catawbas and other piedmont Indians of any blame for the war. Moreover, the Conjurer was willing to fight the Savannahs, Yuchi, and Appalachee, but he refused to fight the Yamassee on the grounds that they were "his ancient people" (Crane 1959: 181). Again we see evidence for cultural and social affiliations between Cherokees and other southeastern Indians.

When Virginia negotiated a treaty with the Catawbas in 1756 at the beginning of the French and Indian war, Haigler, the Catawba leader, made the following statement: "We are in perfect Amity with the Cherokees, Cowetaws, and Chickasaws. The Cherokees have ever been our Friends, and as they are a numerous Nation, we acknowledge them to be our elder Brother" (Anonymous 1906:241). When the English employed Catawbas to fight Cherokees in the French and Indian War, this naturally created enmity between them that lasted for many years. Before the French and Indian War, however, they seem to have been on good terms.

When the Charleston traders succeeded in establishing a direct trade route to the Cherokees, they undermined the position of the Catawba middlemen. In general, the Charleston traders appear to have caused more stress among the Indians than the Virginia traders did. Byrd says that as soon "as the Catawba Indians are inform'd of the Approach of the Virginia Caravans, they send a Detachment of their Warriors to bid them Welcome, and escort them Safe to their Town, Where they are receiv'd with great marks of Distinction." He contrasts the Virginia traders with the Charleston traders.

There are generally some Carolina Traders that constantly live among the Catawbas, and pretend to Exercise a dictatorial Authority over them. These petty Rulers don't only teach the honester Savages all sorts of Debauchery, but are unfair in their dealings, and use them with all kinds of Oppression. Nor has their Behavior been at all better to the rest of the Indian Nations, among whom they reside, by abusing their Women and Evil-entreating their Men; and, by the way, this was the true Reason of the fatal War which the Nations round-about made upon Carolina in the year 1713 (Byrd 1929:302).

Byrd, through his own trade interests, is necessarily biased against the Charleston traders; still he is quite right in saying that they caused a great deal of stress.

Unlike the Virginia traders, the Charleston traders conducted a lively business in Indian slaves. This became so prevalent that in contemporary documents the statement that the Indians had gone to war is virtually synonymous with saying they had gone to capture slaves. According to regulations the Charleston traders were supposed to only buy Indians who had been captured, but this regulation was frequently violated (McDowell 1955:16-17). Sometimes the traders would force their own Indian slaves to go out and capture other Indians for slaves as a means of purchasing their own freedom (McDowell 1955:23).

Another way of motivating Indians to capture slaves was to get them in debt. The commissioners of the Indian trade tried to discourage the sale of rum on this account (McDowell 1955:15). The commissioners also tried to force the traders to contract debts with Indians in the presence of their headmen or kinsmen (McDowell 1955:12). If an Indian failed to pay a debt, his headmen and kinsmen were liable (Mc-Dowell 1955:33-34). This, too, was often violated. Thus, the *modus operandi* of the Charleston trader was to allow Indians to fall heavily in debt (often for rum) and then to force them to go out and capture slaves as a means of paying their debts.

The Virginia and Charleston traders introduced stresses and strains that exceeded the flexibility or "give" of the piedmont tribes and chiefdoms, and when the "give" of a society is exceeded the result may be revolution or, more commonly among primitive people, a nativistic movement. Though the evidence is less than one would wish, it is likely that the "conspiracies" and "wars" on the southern colonial frontier in the late seventeenth and early eighteenth centuries were nativistic movements. For example, a trader residing among the Sewees told Lawson the following story.

They seeing several Ships coming in, to bring the English Supplies from Old England, one chief Part of their Cargo being for a Trade with the Indians, some of the craftiest of them had observed that the Ships came always in at one Place, which made them very confident that Way was the exact Road to England; and seeing so many Ships come thence, they believed it could not be far thither, esteeming the English that were among them, no better than Cheats, and thought, if they could carry the Skins and Furs they got, themselves to England, which were inhabited with a better Sort of People than those sent amongst them, that then they should purchase twenty times the Value for every Pelt they sold Abroad, in Consideration of what Rates they sold for at Home. The intended Barter was exceeding well approved of, and after a general Consultation of the Ablest Heads amongst them it was *Nemine Contradicente* agreed upon, immediately to make in addition to their fleet, by building more Canoes, and those to be of the best Sort and Bigger Size, as for their intended Discovery. Some Indians were employed about making the Canoes, others to hunting, every one to the Post he was most fit for, all Endeavors tending towards an able Fleet and Cargo for Europe. The Affair was carried on with a great deal of Secrecy and Expedition, so as in a small Time they had gotten a Navy, Loading, Provisions, and Hands, ready to set sail leaving only the Old, Impotent and Minors at Home, 'till their successful Return. The Wind presenting, they set up their Mat-Sails, and were scarce out Sight, when there rose a Tempest, which it is supposed carried one Part of these Indian Merchants by Way of the Other World, whilst the others were taken up at Sea, by an English Ship, and sold for Slaves to the Islands. The Remainder are better satisfied with their Imbecilities in such an Undertaking, nothing affronting them more than to reherse their Voyage to England (Lawson 1960:6-7).

William Byrd heard a very suggestive story from the Tuscarora who survived the Tuscarora War of 1711.

These Indians have a very odd Tradition amongst them, that many years ago, their Nation was grown so dishonest, that no man cou'd keep any Goods, or so much as his loving Wife to himself. That, however, their God, being unwilling to root them out for their crimes, did them the honour to send a Messenger from Heaven to instruct them, and set Them a perfect Example of Integrity and kind Behavior towards one another.

But this holy Person, with all his Eloquence and Sanctity of Life, was able to make very little Reformation amongst them. Some few Old Men did listen a little to his Wholesome Advice, but all the Young fellows were quite incorrigible. They not only Neglected his Precepts, but derided and Evil Entreated his Person. At last, taking upon Him to reprove some Young Rakes of the Conechta Clan very sharply for their impiety, they were so provok'd at the Freedom of his Rebukes, that they tied him to a Tree, and shot him with Arrows through the Heart. But their God took instant Vengeance on all who had a hand in the Monstrous Act, by Lightning from Heaven, & has ever since visited their Nation with a continued Train of Calamities, nor will he ever leave off punishing, and wasting their People, till he shall have blotted every living Soul of them out of the World (Byrd 1929:290, 292).

These two instances alone are insufficient evidence for an argument that nativism was widespread among the hill tribes and southern chiefdoms, but one suspects that a further search will turn up additional evidence. Lawson's story, at any rate, is strikingly reminiscent of modern Melanesian cargocult movements. Byrd's story suggests both messianism and anomie.

Lawson mentions several other things suggesting social dysphoria. He says that suicide was not uncommon, "as for Instance, a Bear-River Indian, a very likely young Fellow, about twenty Years of Age, whose Mother was angry at his

drinking of too much Rum, and chid him for it, thereupon
replied, he would have her satisfied, and he would do the like
no more; upon which he made his Words good; for he went
aside, and shot himself dead" (Lawson 1960:214). In addition, their use of alcohol was definitely suicidal. They
would relinquish their most valuable possessions for rum and
then proceed to become as drunk as possible. While drunk
they often injured or killed themselves. Lawson says that
they were aware that alcohol "hurrey (many of them) into
the other World before their Time, as themselves will often
confess" (1960:6). According to Lawson they had a single
word that meant rum, medicine, and poison (1960:252).

Stress was greatest in the sphere of the Charleston traders.
Unlike the Spanish, whose main link with the Indians was
through their missions, the English of Charleston quickly
began to trade with the Indians and to arm them. Under the
Proprietary Government trade regulations were largely in-
effective; the traders could easily circumvent trade regulations and proceed according to their own wishes. Not only
did these traders arm the Indians against the Spanish, they
took advantage of aboriginal political divisions, setting one
group of Indians against others for the purpose of taking
slaves. By 1708 the South Carolinians were using armed
Yamasees to raid southern Florida for slaves; by 1715 Thomas
Nairne claimed to have raided the Florida Keys (Sturtevant
1962:68-70).

The culmination of all this stress came in the Yamasee
War of 1715-16, which Crane characterizes as "a far-reaching
revolt against the Carolinian trading regime, involving the
Creeks, the Choctaw, and to a lesser extent the Cherokee, as
well as the tribes of the piedmont and of the Savannah River
and Port Royal districts" (Crane 1959:162). Eventually the
Yamassees were defeated and handled very severely by the
South Carolinians. The Congarees, Santees, Sewees, Peedees,
Waxhaws, and some Cusabos were said to have been "utterly
extirpated" (Rivers 1885:93). Some of the survivors went to
Florida to take refuge with the Spanish, while others fled
north to live with the Catawbas (Swanton 1922:101-102).

The Yamassee War of 1715-16 marked a turning point in
the history of the Catawbas just as it marked a turning point
in the history of the South Carolina colony. For the Catawbas,

the Yamassee War can be regarded as their last political act from purely native motives and ideology; after this the Catawbas must be regarded as a colonial satellite, a military dependency whose affairs were shaped by the interests of various factions in the colony of South Carolina. For South Carolina, the Yamassee War precipitated the overthrow of rule by the Lords Proprietors in 1719 (Crane 1959:185-186). Subsequently, as South Carolina gradually came under the protection of the crown she enjoyed more autonomy in regulating her own internal affairs and in pursuing her own interests.

Three interests dominated South Carolina politics in the first half of the eighteenth century; the history of the Catawbas cannot be understood apart from these interests. First, the government of South Carolina was interested in encouraging settlement of the back country by European immigrants; these settlers were to serve as a bulwark between the tidewater plantations and the Indians and to offset the alarming increase of Negro slaves. Second, the mercantile faction in Charleston was interested in exploiting the Indians through trade and, of course, in realizing as much profit as possible. Third, the planter faction in Charleston was interested in using trade to gain the allegiance of the Indians for military purposes (Jacobs 1954:3-41).

Inevitably, the simultaneous pursuit of these three interests caused conflict. When European small-scale agriculturalists began settling the middle country and at a somewhat later date the upper country, the Indians were inexorably reduced to such a point that Indian trade became nonexistent. The deepest conflicts, however, emerged from the attempt to use trade as a source of profit and as a means of gaining the allegiance of Indians on the frontier. Even though there were laws designed to prevent the traders from cheating the Indians and from gaining too much control over them, these laws were apparently unenforceable. As we have seen, the Yamassee War was an organized revolt against the Charleston traders.

By 1729 the Charleston traders had successfully undercut the power of the Catawbas; only the Creeks and the Cherokees were a threat to the security of South Carolina. The Creeks maintained their position by becoming something of

an "uncommitted nation," thus remaining intermediate between the Spanish, French, and English (Meriwether 1940:
189-190). The Cherokees maintained their position by living
in a remote, mountainous habitat and by remaining intermediate between the French and the English. We shall see,
however, that the South Carolinians were at this time more
worried about insurrections among Negro slaves than they
were about Indian depredations. Negro slaves constituted
more than two-thirds of the population (Meriwether 1940:6).
As a concrete example of their fears, South Carolinians would
cite the "Stono Insurrection" of 1739 when fifty Negro slaves
revolted, killed twenty-one whites, and fled south in an
attempt to find refuge among the Spanish settlements in
Florida (Meriwether 1940:26).

In the first quarter of the eighteenth century the population of South Carolina was concentrated in the tidewater
area and to a lesser extent in the lower pine belt area, where
the economy had specialized in the production of rice and
indigo. These commodities were produced on plantations that
depended upon large numbers of slaves. To offset the Negro
imbalance and to create a frontier against external danger, the
government encouraged settlement of the middle country,
the upper pine belt stretching to the fall-line. They did this
by encouraging settlement in townships. These townships
were grants of land obtained from the Crown; they were
parceled out to settlers along with tools, stock, and other
encouragements. Between 1733 and 1759, ten of these townships fanned out from Charleston along the rivers and creeks
of the middle country.

The townships that were closest to the Catawbas were
the Congarees Township on the Congaree and Saluda Rivers,
the Fredericksburg Township on the Wateree River, and the
Queensboro Township on the Peedee River. Like the Indians
before them, these settlers were interested in settling on the
rivers and creeks; this was partly for transportation but more
for the rich land along the river bottoms. Around 1737, for
example, a man named John Thompson who traded with the
Indians on the Peedee River "bought" their lands. His purchase included "about forty 'old fields' as the abandoned
cleared lands of the Indians were called" (Meriwether 1940:
92-93).

In addition to the protection offered by the townships, the South Carolina government sought to enlist the allegiance of the Catawbas and other Indians through trade. After the Yamassee War a "fort and factory" were established and maintained between 1717 and 1722 on the Congaree River near the present city of Columbia. At this point, the trading path from Charleston branched into a trail leading to the Cherokees and a trail leading to the Catawbas (Crane 1959: 188). As a safeguard against further uprisings like the Yamassee War, in 1716 the planter faction wrested the Indian trade out of the hands of the merchants, making it a public monopoly. After the trade became a public monopoly, they attempted to force the Indians to come to the factories to trade. For the Catawbas this meant going to the Congaree Factory, where the trade was in the hands of Eleazer Wigan, and later Captain James How (Crane 1959:193). This proved, however, to be very unpopular with the Catawbas, and it gave the Virginia traders an open field. In 1717 Wigan complained that Virginians with trains of pack-horses were undercutting him by selling cheaper goods to the Catawbas; in reply, he was instructed to lower his prices even if it entailed a loss to the public. Later a similar arrangement was made with the Cherokee Indians (Crane 1959:196-197).

Even though it meant defeating the planters who wanted trade to be used for defense, the mercantile faction eventually succeeded in dissolving the monopoly; the trade again became private in 1721 (Crane 1959:198-199). Consequently the South Carolinians were again faced with the problem of regulating private traders. In an attempt to do this, an act was passed in 1731 requiring that each trader be licensed to trade in a particular "Nation" or village; each trader was further required to visit Charleston once every twelve or eighteen months to renew his license. On this license the trader could specify the names of two white assistants (Crane 1959:198-199).

The trade with the Catawbas gradually fell into the hands of traders resident in the townships. After 1735, John Thompson traded with the "Cheraw Indians" living on the east bank of the Peedee River. Later traders in this area were Samuel Armstrong, Christopher Gadsden, and John Crawford, all of whom probably traded with Indians as well as with whites. The Wateree Township occupied the old fields used by the Wateree Indians before the Yamassee uprising. Even though the Waterees objected to settlement on their lands there still was trade. The most important Wateree trader was Samuel Wyley, who established a store and inn around 1751; subsequently he became an unofficial but effective agent to the Catawbas (Meriwether 1940:90-104).

However, the most important center of Catawba trade was in the Congaree township near the old garrison and factory. The most important Congaree trader was Thomas Brown, who established a trading post around 1730. Associated with him were Alexander Kilpatrick and Thomas' brother Patrick who became an important trader among the Creeks after 1740 (Meriwether 1940:53). After the Catawbas were decimated by a severe smallpox epidemic in 1738, Brown's fortunes declined; in 1747 he died, heavily in debt. After Brown's death the Catawba trade was taken over by Robert Steill and others. The center for Cherokee trade shifted north to a settlement known as "Ninety Six," where it was under the control of Robert Geiger; after his death it was taken over by Robert Goudey (Meriwether 1940:63).

Throughout the 1730's and 1740's there was a trickle of trade from Virginia, but the Charleston traders were dominant. Their power was both economic and political. For example, George Haig, a Carolina trader to the Catawbas and the Cherokees, persuaded the Catawbas in 1742 to yield one of their men who had ravished a white woman (Meriwether 1940:58).

The Catawbas apparently began to adopt English surnames during this period. Thomas Brown had a son by a Catawba woman around 1730. This son, also named Thomas Brown, apparently lived among the Catawbas (Meriwether 1940: 53). In 1748, while George Haig and the younger Thomas Brown were on a trip to the Catawbas they were seized by Iroquois and taken north. Conrad Weiser, the noted northern Indian agent, was able to ransom young Brown, but he learned that Haig had tired and his captors were forced to kill him. Brown is today one of the most frequent names among modern Catawbas.

The means by which the Charleston traders gained control of the Catawbas can be seen in the writings of Edmund Atkin, who was once a trader himself. Drawing on his own experience, he devised a plan in 1755 to control the activities of the traders. Atkin takes pains to point out that the laws of South Carolina did not effectively control the traders. The traders usurped the power of the Indian elders by rewarding the young men, the ones who were most productive for their trade. The traders then gained control over these younger men by allowing them to fall heavily in their debt. In addition, the traders were able to conceal their knowledge of Indian affairs from officials in Charleston, or even to send them misleading information. Atkins notes that the practice of getting Indians in debt often backfired because they sometimes revolted as a means of canceling their debts (Jacobs 1954:23-29).

In the 1740's the South Carolina government considered the Catawbas to be a "nation." In contrast to small "tribes" and families living among the settlements, a nation was a group of Indians who were numerous and had lands of their own (Glen 1951:60). The "settlement Indians" consisted of Charraws (Sara), Uchees (Yuchi), Peedees, Notches (Natchez), Cape Fears, and others (Gregg 1867:14). Writing in 1746, Governor James Glen says that the Catawbas had about 300 fighting men. The Catawbas, along with the Cherokee, Chickasaw, Creek, and Choctaw Nations, formed the western political boundary of South Carolina (Glen 1951:12).

Glen gives the impression that the Catawbas were a wholly independent, organized, homogeneous people with sovereignty over their territory. That this was not the case can be seen in the writings of James Adair, a trader who knew them better. Adair's figure for the Catawba population in 1743 is 400 fighting men (1930:235). This is only a hundred more than Glen's figure; not greatly different as early estimates of population go.

However, the resemblance between Adair's and Glen's descriptions of the Catawbas ends with these population estimates. Adair says that there were over *twenty* "dialects" spoken in the Catawba Nation. He gives the names of a few: "*Katahba,* is the standard or court-dialect, the *Wataree,* who make up a large town; *Eeno, Chewah,* now *Chowan, Cang-*

garee, Nachee, Yamassee, Coosah, &c" (1930:235-236). One
wishes that Adair's list were longer. If it were, it would
probably show that languages representing every major
linguistic stock in the eastern United States were spoken by
"Catawba" Indians. One thing, however, is clear: the Catawba
"Nation" of the 1740's was a composite group made up of
refugees from broken societies.

Adair describes the territory of the Catawbas as having
very good soil and resources.

The land would produce any sort of Indian provisions,
but, by the continual passing and repassing of the English,
between the northern and southern colonies, the Katahba live
perhaps the meanest of any Indians belonging to the British
American empire. They are also so corrupted by an immoderate
use of our spiritous liquors, and of course, indolent, that they
scarcely plant any thing fit for the support of human life.
South-Carolina has supplied their wants, either through a political,
or charitable view; which kindness, several respectable inhabitants
in their neighborhood say, they abuse in a very high degree;
for they often destroy the white people's live stock, and even
kill their horses for mischief sake (Adair 1930:234).

Not only were they not homogeneous, they were not self-
sufficient. They depended on South Carolina, at least in
part, for their food and clothing.

Edmond Atkin, writing in 1755, says that the Catawbas had
about 320 fighting men (Jacobs 1954:42). At this time Atkin
makes it clear that the Catawbas were "directed intirely
[*sic*] by the Government of So. Carolina." In recent years
they had been on bad terms with the Shawnee, Cherokee,
Iroquois, and others. To add to their troubles, surveyers,
particularly Virginians and North Carolinians, were violating
the South Carolina law which made it illegal to survey within
thirty miles of Catawba lands. Because they were reduced to
a small number and surrounded on all sides by white settlers,
the Catawbas considered moving to the lower Creek Nation
(Jacobs 1954:46-48).[6]

6. In 1752 the Catawbas appealed to Governor Glen to strengthen them
by encouraging some of the settlement Indians (Peedees) to move up and
join them (Gregg 1867:13-14). In 1760, reduced to only 75 men, the
Catawbas wanted to move nearer to the coast. They consented to remain
on the frontier when the government of South Carolina promised to build
them a fort (Salley 1929:20-21).

When the French and Indian War (in the south, the "Cherokee War") broke out, the Catawbas were reluctant to become overt enemies of the Cherokees, who had aligned themselves with the French. However, by one means or another they were persuaded to serve under Lyttleton and Bull in their Cherokee campaigns (Jacobs 1954:47). In Lyttleton's expedition of 1759-60, a smallpox epidemic broke out and about half of his Catawba warriors died. In 1760 William Bull equipped about forty Catawbas and moved their families south to the English settlement at Pine Tree Hill for protection. Later in the year the Catawbas produced a prisoner and several Cherokee scalps for payment. Still later in that same year, the province built a fort for the Catawbas on their lands, and their families subsequently left Pine Tree Hill and returned home. In December of 1761 the Cherokees signed a treaty in Charleston ending the hostilities.

As the middle country townships were filling up, a trickle of settlers also filtered into the piedmont, although their numbers were limited owing to the Cherokees and other Indians who occasionally raided them. Just before the Cherokee War, several settlers were located on Stevens Creek and in the Saluda River Valley. At a somewhat slower rate settlers filtered into the upper Broad River Valley. Although Governor Glen prohibited surveys within 30 miles of the Catawbas, this continued to be violated by frontiersmen from Virginia and North Carolina. By the time of the Cherokee War there were around 500 settlers in the Waxhaws region and about 300 in the vicinity of Rocky Creek and Fishing Creek. The Catawbas resented intrusions upon their land and in one known instance drove a settler from Fishing Creek and burned his home. Primarily, these back country settlers were subsistence agriculturists who supplemented their agriculture by hunting and fishing. Apparently the economy of the frontiersmen was similar to the economy of the piedmont Indians (Meriwether 1940:117-240).

Because of Indian raids and the Cherokee War, the back country filled up slowly. After the Cherokee War, however, settlers came in great numbers. Between 1761 and 1765 the population of the piedmont increased by 50 per cent. Many of the settlers came from Pennsylvania, Virginia, and North

Carolina. The piedmont developed into a distinct region—
a continuation of piedmont society in the north—with con-
nections with the tidewater and middle country regions that
were tenuous at best. "The tidewater and back country were
indeed two commonwealths, one highly developed, cultivated
and confident; the other new, raw, slightly organized and
uncertain of itself" (Meriwether 1940:261). The way of
life of the frontiersmen was sharply different from that of the
low country planters.

In 1763 the Catawbas were still thought by some to be an
independent nation. George Milligen-Johnston was of the
opinion that the Indians by nature would not allow themselves to be subjects of Britain; their relationship was that of
friend or brother.

> . . . certain it is that they are not subject to our Laws; that
> they have no Magistrates appointed over them by our Kings;
> that they have no Representatives in our Assemblies; that their
> own Consent is necessary to engage them in War on our Side;
> and that they have the Power of Life and Death, Peace and
> War, in their own Councils, without being accountable to us;
> Subjection is what they are unacquainted with in their own
> State, there being no such Thing as coercive Power among them:
> their Chiefs are such only in Virtue of their Credit, and not
> their Power; there being, in all other Circumstances, a perfect
> Equality among them (1951:185-186).

Perhaps Milligen-Johnston was able to hold this view by
living in Charleston at a respectable distance from the
Catawbas.

Under the direction of John Stuart, the Superintendent
of Indian Affairs for the southern district, a Congress was
held at Augusta, Georgia, in November 1763 (Alden 1944:
183). Attended by the Catawbas, Chickasaws, Choctaws,
Creeks, and Cherokees, the Congress had as its purpose the
settlement of grievances after the French and Indian War.
Because Haigler had been killed two months earlier, a man
named Colonel Ayers was elected "King" of the Catawbas
at the Congress. The Catawbas, complaining of white encroachments and a lack of hunting territory, asked for a
reservation of thirty square miles. However, in the final
treaty they were granted a reservation of fifteen square miles

and they were promised their former hunting rights outside of that area (Meriwether 1940:245).

Subsequently, Colonel Ayers apparently fell out of favor with the South Carolina government. Acting on behalf of Governor Bull, Samuel Wyly supervised a meeting of the Catawbas in January 1765; in Ayer's place "King Frow" was elected. The names of his headmen were Captain Thomson, John Chestnut, and Wateree Jenny (Kirkland and Kennedy 1905:56-57).

After the Cherokee War, the Catawbas were too decimated to be of much military importance. Although they contributed a few warriors to fight against the British in the American Revolution, the importance of their participation was rather negligible. At the close of the eighteenth century, the low country South Carolinians still considered the Catawbas to be a nation, a military dependency. Yet it is obvious that they were of negligible military importance. The Catawba "Nation" consisted of about a hundred Indians maintaining a desperate existence on a reservation of fifteen square miles. On all sides they were surrounded by Scotch-Irish frontiersmen whose numbers increased at an alarming rate. What these frontiersmen wanted was land, and they did not need Indians to protect them from other Indians. The conclusion is clear: at the turn of the nineteenth century the Catawbas were socially anomalous; they were not what they were supposed to be.

CHAPTER IV

The Catawbas in a Plural Society

As THE nineteenth century drew nearer, the Catawbas became an increasingly anomalous social group. They were a handful of Indians but were called a "nation," and they occupied fifteen square miles of valuable land surrounded on all sides by thousands of land-hungry, Scotch-Irish frontiersmen whose number increased daily. However, this anomaly was more apparent than real. The social position of the late eighteenth century Catawbas seems anomalous because we have been examining the history of their "international" relations with the tacit assumption that they were an independent society. The fact is that the independence of the Catawbas underwent a gradual attrition throughout the eighteenth century, particularly after the Cherokee War.

The social position of the Catawbas in the late eighteenth and early nineteenth centuries was that of a sociocultural section in a plural society. J. S. Furnivall, who first used the concept of "plural society" in a technical sense, cites as an example of a plural society the case of colonial Burma, where there was a medley of peoples that mixed but did not combine. "There is a plural society, with different sections of the community living side by side, but separately, within the same political unit" (Furnivall 1948:304).

Developing the concept more rigorously, M. G. Smith specifies that a society must meet three conditions to be classified as plural (1960:763). First, it must include two or more cultural sections whose core institutions differ.[1]

---

1. Smith follows Malinowski in defining an institution as an interdependent system of action, idea and value, and social relations. Core

(Continued on facing page)

Second, these cultural sections must also be social sections. That is, there must be little or no circulation of people from one cultural section to another, and relationships between people in the different sections must be specific, segmental, and governed by structural factors. Third, and most important, one of these cultural sections, usually a minority, must have a monopoly on power.[2] Having a vested interest in the *status quo*, this minority tends to discourage acculturation by sponsoring an ideology that maintains the divisions within the system (Smith 1960:767-775).

Throughout the nineteenth century (and perhaps part of the twentieth century) South Carolina meets the conditions of Smith's definition. In order to understand the Catawbas of this period, it is necessary to view them as a sociocultural section within a plural society. Seen in this light, it is easier to understand why the Catawbas remained a distinctive people even when most of their aboriginal cultural patterns were gone. For example, when their culture was almost defunct, they bolstered their distinctiveness by becoming Mormons, even though local whites exerted considerable pressure to discourage them from doing so (Hicks 1964).

Not only was nineteenth century South Carolina a plural society, but like the rest of the South it was what economists now call an underdeveloped society. This was true as late as 1938, when the South was characterized by "inadequate housing, education and health facilities, an agriculture characterized by absentee ownership, single-crop farming, underemployment, and per capita incomes under $200 a year" (Goldschmidt 1963).

In 1763, when the Catawbas were granted their fifteen square-mile reservation at the Augusta Congress, South Carolina society was composed of three cultural sections. These were Europeans, Southern Indians, and African Negroes in

---

institutions are kinship, education, religion, property and economy, recreation, and certain sodalities (Smith 1960:767-769).

Peter Carstens has called my attention to some remarkable parallels between the position of the Catawbas in South Carolina in the recent past and that of certain of the "coloured people" in South Africa. The interested reader should see Marais (1962) and especially Carstens (1966).

2. Government and class are not core institutions. It is within the framework of these institutions that cultural differences exist.

various stages of acculturation.[3] These three cultural sections were cross-cut by social divisions into several distinct sociocultural sections, which in turn were internally divided into status hierarchies.[4] It was an exceedingly complex society which, as we shall see, was neither integrated nor in equilibrium. In the following pages, I shall discuss only the sociocultural sections that are necessary for an understanding of the position of the Catawbas in the larger society.

The low country Europeans constituted the sociocultural section that had a monopoly on power. Specifically, all effective economic and political power lay in the hands of a small number of planters who occupied the apex of the low country European status hierarchy. The prestige of a planter was measured by the number of slaves he possessed and the size of his plantation, these being indices of the amount of rice and indigo he could produce. Because plantation life was lonely and because it exposed one to malaria and other diseases, the wealthier planters lived in Charleston for part of the year. Those who could afford it lived there the year around, being absentee owners in the true sense (Wallace 1951:195).

Below the planters there was a middle class composed of professionals and merchants, many of the latter having an interest in the Indian trade. This middle class was both small and insecure, as is often the case in preindustrial societies. When there was a conflict of interest between the planters and the middle class, the planters usually prevailed. We have seen, for example, that the planters were able to temporarily take the Indian trade away from these merchants, making it a public monopoly. The planters regarded the middle class as necessary, perhaps, but socially inferior.

Occupying the bottom rung of the low country European status hierarchy, there was a lower class composed of a few servants, artisans, and yeomen, the latter being farmers who owned no slaves. These yeomen practiced a diversified sub-

3. The Europeans were primarily English, Irish, and Scotch, though there were a few French, Swiss, and Germans.

4. The sociocultural sections of a plural society may contain internal status continua, while the sections themselves need not be ranked in a hierarchy (Smith 1960:769).

sistence agriculture on land that was unsuitable for the production of rice and indigo. In addition to agriculture, they commonly hunted and fished to supplement their food supply.

In addition to these low country Europeans, after the Cherokee War thousands of European settlers left Pennsylvania, Virginia and North Carolina to settle the South Carolina Piedmont. These frontiersmen, like the low country yeomen, usually did not own slaves. They were also similar to the yeomen in practicing subsistence agriculture supplemented by hunting and fishing. Many of them were mobile: they would settle for a few years and then move further south and west in hopes of getting better land in newer territory. Even though the European population of the piedmont quickly surpassed that of the low country, the piedmont frontiersmen at first had very little political power. All important decisions were made by the planters.

Virtually all of the African Negroes were slaves; the main exceptions were a few free Negroes who won their manumission through purchase or meritorious acts. In the nineteenth century manumission became increasingly difficult; finally, in 1820 a law was passed forbidding manumission. The social institutions of the Negro slaves were, of course, different from those of the Europeans. They were culturally heterogeneous, coming from quite diverse African cultures. Their masters made an explicit effort to keep them from organizing as a means of preventing insurrections and conspiracies. In 1762, for example, one estimate was that out of 46,000 slaves, only 500 were Christians. The whites were afraid that if the Negroes became their Christian brothers they would want their freedom as well (Wallace 1951:183-184). In addition to his exclusion from the Christian brotherhood, a slave had no economic or political power; he could not be legally married, and he could be beaten as severely as his master wished. As Elkins (1963) has argued, American slavery was the severest the world has even seen.

The third cultural section, the Southern Indians, consisted of people who were incorporated into plural South Carolina in three ways. First, as we have already seen, many Indians were enslaved. The Charleston traders, taking advantage of existing cultural and social differences, played one group against another as a means of acquiring slaves. Francis Le Jau, writing in 1711-1712, tells of one trader who brought in approximately a hundred Indian slaves at one time (Klingberg 1956:109). These were mostly women and children. Adult male Indians were a threat to the security of the colony because they could escape and carry intelligence to other Indians. As a consequence, adult males were generally tortured to death by their Indian captors (Klingberg 1956: 116, 122-123).

Second, there were a number of "free" or "settlement" Indians who lived a rather impoverished existence among the English settlements near the coast. Le Jau, a missionary, attempted to persuade some of these settlement Indians to live with him, "but they will not consent to it, nor part with their Children tho' they lead miserably poor lives" (Klingberg 1956:41). "They were allowed to goe their own way and bring up their children like themselves" (Kingberg 1956:109). Le Jau says that because they laid up no provisions they were always on the move in search of food. Some of the children spoke English, while their parents did not. Le Jau mentions some of these settlement Indians having "gone further up in the Country thro' badd usage they received from some of Our People." The settlement Indians were detribalized; owning no land they hunted and performed petty services for the colonists.

The third way that Indians were incorporated into plural South Carolina was as "national" Indians. As we have seen, Indians were said to be a nation when they were numerous and had lands of their own. The Catawbas, however, were an exception in that they were few in number while occupying only fifteen square miles of land and were threatened by the thousands of frontiersmen surrounding them.

This anomaly is explained when we see that there were two **reasons** why the Catawbas had a position in the plural society. For one thing, the Scotch-Irish frontiersmen of the piedmont had no political power; the decision to grant the Catawbas a reservation was made by the low country planters, for whom piedmont land was at that time of little value. A second and more positive reason was that the low country planters had a use for the Catawbas. As we have seen, there was a great disproportion of Negroes and whites in the middle of the eighteenth century, and the whites were in constant fear of slaves escaping and conspiring to do violence. The effect of this on the Indians appears as early as 1716, at a meeting of the Board of Indian Commissioners of South Carolina.

Mr. Barthm. Gaillard informed the Board, that some of the Wineau Indians were seated at Santee, and have been found beneficial to that Part of this Province, for their Safety, by keeping the Negroes there in Awe, and desired us to take that Matter into Consideration, and proposed the Settling a small factory there, to ingage those Indians to continue among them, and further offered to manage that Trade gratis (McDowell 1955: 80).

The fear of violence, conspiracies, and insurrections on the part of Negro slaves increased as time went on. George Milligen-Johnston, writing in 1763, states the planters' need for the Indians even more clearly.

They (the Negro slaves) are in this Climate necessary, but very dangerous Domestics, their Number so much exceeding the Whites; a natural Dislike and Antipathy, that subsists between them and our *Indian* Neighbors, is a very lucky Circumstance, and for this Reason: In our Quarrels with the *Indians*, however proper and necessary it may be to give them Correction, it can never be to our Interest to extirpate them, or to force them from their Lands; their Ground would be soon taken up by runaway Negroes from our Settlements, whose Numbers would daily increase, and quickly become more formidable Enemies than *Indians* can ever be, as they speak our Language and would never be at a loss for Intelligence (Milligen-Johnston 1951:136).[5]

For the planters, it was comforting to think that the Negroes were terrified by Indians, particularly by those Indians who, like the Catawbas, were situated at some distance from the settlements.

---

5. In addition to indicating the planters' need for the Indians, this passage suggests that the palnters had mixed feelings toward Negro acculturation. Acculturation made them more efficient as workers, but more dangerous as enemies.

In 1769 Governor Montagu, in presenting his case for establishing the boundary between North and South Carolina, pointed out the imbalance of Negroes and whites in South Carolina. For this reason he wanted the Catawbas on the South Carolina side of the boundary.

The year 1766 afforded a very strong proof of their Utility, on such services, for about the Christmas of 1765 many Negroes having fled into large Swamps, and other circumstances concurring, there was a great room to apprehend that some dangerous conspiracy and insurrection was intended, and tho' the Militia was ordered on duty and were very alert on this occasion, the Governor thought it proper also to invite a number of the Catawba Indians to come down and hunt the negroes in their different recesses almost impervious to White Men at that Season of the Year. The Indians immediately came and partly by the Terror of their name, their diligence and singular sagacity in pursuing Enemies through such Thickets soon dispersed the runaway Negroes, apprehended several and most of the rest of them chose to surrender themselves to their Masters, & return to their duty rather than Expose themselves to the attack of an Enemy so dreaded and so difficult to be resisted or evaded, for which good service the Indians were very amply rewarded (Salley 1929:27).

The Catawbas in the late eighteenth century occupied their social position by virtue of the role that the planters *thought* they played. As we shall presently see, there are grounds for doubting that they played this role effectively.

In the latter half of the eighteenth century, the Catawbas are generally described as being a small nation, but a very fierce and loyal nation. This was precisely what the planters wanted. Being few in number, the Catawbas could not bargain with the colonists by using threats of hostility. They were loyal, meaning they were under the *de facto* control of the whites. But most important they had the reputation of being fierce, thus hopefully keeping the Negro slaves in awe.

The use of Indians to intimidate slaves was only one of the devices used by slave owners. For example, when Frederick Olmstead was touring the Southern back country a few years before the Civil War, a threatening rain cloud forced him to take shelter near a house. The man of the house called seven Negro children out to see Olmstead's dog, Jude.

"Just look a here! here's a reg'lar nigger dog; have it to
ketch niggers when they run away, or don't behave." (He got
a piece of bread and threw it to Jude.) "There! did you see
that! See what teeth she's got, she'd just snap a nigger's leg off.
. . . it'll snap a nigger's head right off, just as easy as you'd take a
chicken's head off with an ax" (Olmstead 1959:216-217).

The bloodhounds in *Uncle Tom's Cabin* seem to have played
much the same role. Though primarily used for tracking,
their ferociousness was always played up and often exaggerated.

It may be that the ferociousness of the Catawbas, particularly in the last quarter of the eighteenth century, was
like that of bloodhounds: exaggerated. When John Symth
(1784: Vol. I, 118-124) visited the Catawbas in the early
1780's, white people living in the area told him that the
Catawbas were not like other Indians. Smyth describes them
as being perhaps more docile and servile than lower class
whites. He estimated that they had about 60 to 70 warriors.
They lived in "wigwams," but they were well on their way
to being acculturated. The Catawba "King" had an Indian
name, but he was also called "Joe." The latter spoke English
"very intelligibly"; he told Smyth that most of the Catawbas
spoke English as well as their own language.

Smyth says that divorce was easy among the Catawbas, and
promiscuous intercourse was allowed. Unmarried women
often committed abortions, and a woman generally had
only two or three children during her life. Smyth noted
that when white men lived on the reservation, even if it were
only for a few months, they had a wigwam built and took
an Indian woman to serve as wife and servant. These white
men were sometimes adopted into the nation and given an
allotment of land to use.

At the time of Smyth's visit Catawba women appear to
have been more productive than Catawba men. They raised
gardens and made baskets, mats, and pottery to sell to whites.
The men seem to have concentrated on hunting and fishing.
When they had the means they were reputed to drink ex-
cessive amounts of alcoholic beverages, often becoming violent
when intoxicated. Smyth says that when a woman became
aware that her husband was drinking, she quickly hid every-

thing that might be used to inflict injury on another person. Men under the influence of alcohol were not held responsible for anything they did; it was blamed on alcohol.

The details of Catawba culture at the end of the eighteenth century escape us. Most of the ethnography on the Catawbas was done after 1900.[6] Because most of the cultural patterns in this ethnography were drawn from the memory of elderly informants, we cannot be certain when they were viable. However, we can be relatively sure that the Catawbas were still a cultural section in the closing years of the eighteenth century. In addition, one further thing is relatively certain: from Smyth's observations we see that the Catawbas of the late eighteenth century were not as ferocious as they were made out to be. Subsequently this became increasingly apparent, and their position in the larger society changed accordingly.

The social position of the Catawbas in the late eighteenth century was partly determined by ecological factors. At that time, valuable land was land that was suitable for growing rice and indigo. Consequently the only valuable land was that in the low country plantations, the owners of which were the dominant minority in the society. The planters who were responsible for granting the Catawbas fifteen square miles of piedmont land probably felt that it was a small favor. The planters owed nothing to the frontiersmen, but they did owe something to the Catawbas.

Still, the Catawbas began to feel the pressure of these frontiersmen within two decades after they were granted the reservation. When Smyth visited the Catawbas after the Revolutionary War, some of them told him about their fear of whites coming in and taking over (1784:Vol. I, 124). The Catawbas were few in number, and they were becoming even fewer. For this reason, perhaps, they sometimes adopted white men into the nation and allowed them to use certain tracts of land (Smyth 1784:Vol. I, 122). This was probably the way in which Thomas Spratt, supposedly the first white

---

6. In addition to references already cited, the reader may want to refer to work by Vladimir J. Fewkes (1944), M. R. Harrington (1908), John R. Swanton (1918), and the extensive research of Frank G. Speck.

man to become a permanent resident with the Catawbas, was able to establish himself. He is thought to have settled there around 1763 (Brown 1953:60-61). Like other white men before him Spratt subsequently gained considerable power and influence over the Catawbas.

In 1782 the Catawbas appealed to Congress to secure their land against alienation by force, even when it was with their own consent. Since the federal government had never signed a treaty with the Catawbas, Congress passed a resolution recommending that South Carolina secure their holdings (Scaife 1896:9). However, these measures did not alleviate the fears of the Catawbas. In 1791 George Washington took his southern tour, and while staying at the home of a Mr. Crawford who lived near the reservation, Washington was approached by several chiefs of the Catawbas. They again repeated their fears of being alienated from their land by whites (Salley 1932:282ff).

In the early years of the nineteenth century, the two foundations of the social position of the Catawbas in plural South Carolina rapidly eroded. The image of Catawba ferociousness changed, and the low country rice-indigo economy changed. It became more and more apparent that the Catawbas were not fierce savages who could be used to intimidate Negro slaves. In one of his short stories, William Gilmore Simms tells of Catawbas who used to come from their reservation to Charleston every spring to sell pottery. They would break up into small groups—like "European Gipseys" —and filter down the Edisto and Ashley Rivers, camping along the way. Once in the vicinity of Charleston, they would dig clay and fire their pottery. Simms' story hinges on the attempt of a Negro slave driver, Mingo, to seduce Caloya, a Catawba woman. Mingo confronts Caloya's male companion, Knuckles, and tells him that he does not hold with Indians making their women do most of the work. He also tells Knuckles that he is not afraid of him or any other Indian. "How you talk, Knuckles! Wha make you better for fight than me! Ki, man! Once you stan' afore Mingo, you tumble. . . . Neber Indian kin stan' agen black man, whedder for fight or work. . . . You can't fight fair and you can't work. You aint got streng' for it" (Simms n.d.:

386). Mingo's designs are upset when his master, an up-
standing young planter, steps in and demotes him from his
job as driver. The following year the planter allows all of
the Catawbas to camp and dig clay in the "Red Gulley," a
clay pit on his plantation (Simms n.d.:429).[7]

Not only were the Negroes losing their fear of Indians,
the whites were also changing their ideas about them. The first
half of the nineteenth century was the hey day of the ro-
mantic historical novelists, of whom Sir Walter Scott, James
Fenimore Cooper, and William Gilmore Simms were fore-
most. It was also the hey day of Indian dramas; these were
particularly popular between 1820 and 1840 (Holman 1961:
xiii). The most famous of these dramas, *Metamora*, was probably seen by more Americans than was *Tobacco Road* or
Abie's Irish Rose in this century (Hallowell 1957:208).

In the nineteenth century the whites began to speak
of the Catawbas as children of nature. Having a simple and
generous nature, they were unable to cope with the com-
plexities and temptations of civilization. This was the view
of Robert Mills, an articulate South Carolina surveyor.

Had the Indians of this country been of a ferocious and
jealous character, their numbers would have enabled them to
frustrate all attempts of Europe to colonize the country; but so
widely different was their character from this, that like children
of nature, (as they were), they received the whites with kindness, gave them as much land as they wanted, and every assistance in supplying them with provisions (Mills 1826:104).

The image of the Catawbas changed from the fierce but
loyal savage to the noble but childlike savage.

Mills was in favor of giving assistance to the Catawbas
in repayment for their generosity. At the same time, however,
he argued that South Carolina should reclaim the Catawba
reservation.

A right to the soil of the country was grounded upon the
acknowledged truth of this doctrine, that the earth was made
for man; and was intended by the Creator of all things to be

---

7. Simms was an ante-bellum Southern writer in the tradition of James
Fenimore Cooper (cf. Holman 1961:vii-xx). Presumably, his story takes
place in the second decade of the nineteenth century.

improved for the benefit of mankind. The land which could support one savage, in his mode of living, is capable of supporting five hundred, under proper cultivation. These wild lands, therefore, were not the separate property of a few savages who hunted over them, but belonged to the common stock of mankind. The first who possessed a vacant spot, and actually cultivated it for some time, ought to be considered as the proprietor of that spot, and they who derive their titles from him have a valid right to the same (Mills 1826:106).

Thus, the Catawbas being hunters were savages; they were different from those who could properly cultivate the soil to "the benefit of mankind."[8]

In addition to a change in image, the nineteenth century brought in another change that eventually alienated the Catawbas from their reservation. In 1785 cotton was experimentally grown in the vicinity of Charleston. However, it was the invention of the cotton gin in 1793 that reshaped the economy of South Carolina, and with it most of the South. Around 1800, cotton was introduced into the piedmont. As low country planters moved inland to obtain piedmont land, many of the frontiersmen moved further west. These planters brought their slaves with them, and they imported additional slaves at an astonishing rate. In 1800, 15.6 percent of the total population of the Southern Piedmont were slaves; in 1850, 35.0 percent were slaves, an increase of 124 percent (Tang 1958:24-25).

Piedmont land was no longer regarded as land fit only for Indians and frontiersmen. In 1808 South Carolina passed an act making it "expedient" that the Catawbas should have the right to lease their lands. According to the act, their lands were to be leased for terms not exceeding 99 years. All leases were to be witnessed by a majority of five superintendents, appointed by the governor, and "signed and sealed by at least four of the head men or chiefs of the said Catawba Indians" (Brevard 1814:Vol. I, title 96).

---

8. By the nineteenth century the whites almost universally thought of American Indians as being non-agricultural hunters. The reasons for the emergence of this stereotype are not clear. Quite probably the stereotype is a mixture of fact and fiction. That is, the Indians may have practiced less agriculture because of trade, and the Indian was pictured as a savage hunter as part of the rationale for alienating him from his land.

By 1826 the Catawbas, about 30 families or 110 individuals in all, were living in two villages. The largest, Newtown, seems to have been located on the west bank of the Catawba River; the other, Turkeyhead, was on the opposite side of the river. They had leased out their land in 300 acre portions, receiving $15 to $20 per year for each portion. Mills estimates that this would have brought in about $5,000 per year all told, enough to support the Catawbas comfortably. "Yet these wretched Indians live in a state of abject poverty, the consequence of their indolence and dissipated habits. They dun for their rent before it is due, and the $10 or $20 received are frequently spent in debauch; poverty, beggary, and misery follow for a year" (Mills 1826:114).

In 1839 Governor Noble of South Carolina appointed a commission to negotiate with the Catawbas to cede their lands. These commissioners were John Springs, D. Hutchison, E. Avery, B. L. Massey, and Allen Morrow, at least some of whom themselves leased lands on the reservation. In their report they say that every foot of land was leased out. The Catawbas had dwindled to 12 men, 36 women, and 40 children—88 in all, nine of whom were a family of Pamunkeys from Virginia (Scaife 1896:10).[9] In recent years, the Catawbas had been "wandering through the country, forming kind of camps, without any homes, houses, or fixed residence, and destitute of any species of property save dogs and a few worthless horses" (Scaife 1896:11). The commissioners also report there were 500 to 600 white families living on leased land. The original tracts had been subdivided into smaller tracts, and no regular record of the transactions had been kept.

On March 13, 1840, these commissioners signed a treaty with the Catawbas. The Cawtabas agreed to cede their lands in return for the following: (1) the State of South Carolina would furnish them a tract of land worth $5,000, to be purchased in Haywood County, N. C., or in some other mountainous or thinly populated region; (2) If no satisfactory

9. A "woman" was probably a female who had given birth to children. The sexual disproportion suggests that the family structure was either polygynous or matrifocal; in view of their poverty, it was probably the latter.

lands were to be had, they were to be paid $5,000 in cash; (3) Upon removal, the Catawbas were to be paid $2,500 and the sum of $1,500 per year for nine years afterwards (Scaife 1896:12).

Apparently South Carolina made none of these promises good until ten or twenty years after the treaty was signed. The historical record is obscure. It is clear, however, that some person or agency at some time gave back to the Catawbas a reservation of approximately 630 acres of their original reservation.[10] It is also clear that the State of South Carolina subsequently assumed the responsibility of administering this reservation, and "a number of years" before 1893 began giving the Catawbas an annual "pension" of $800, appointing agents to handle their affairs (Scaife 1896:13).

It is also known that in 1840, the year the treaty was signed, "about one hundred Catawba, nearly all that were left of the tribe being dissatisfied with their condition in South Carolina, moved up in a body and took up their residence with the Cherokee" (Mooney 1900:165). The motive that impelled the Catawbas to leave South Carolina could have been dissatisfaction or force or both. We do not know whether *all* of the Catawbas moved to Cherokee, or only the majority of them. In addition, we do not know what motive impelled the Cherokees to accept them; perhaps the Catawbas promised them some of the money that South Carolina had promised to pay.

Apparently, conflict broke out between the Catawbas and Cherokees. In 1848 the Bureau of Indians Affairs received a letter from the Catawbas at Cherokee requesting that an official be appointed to organize their removal to the west.[11] The letter was signed by Chief William Morrison and the heads of all Catawba families.[12] Apparently the Catawbas

---

10. Modern Catawbas tell two stories concerning this transaction. Some say that the Old Reservation was given to them by the state; others say that it was given to them by a sympathetic individual, a Mr. White.

11. *The Catawba Tribe of Indians*, Senate Document No. 144, 54th Congress, 2nd session, February 3, 1897, p. 8.

12. There are a total of 42 "heads of families." If these are actually heads of families, there is marked sexual disproportion; judging from the names, only 15 of the heads of families were male while 27 were female. One of my Catawba informants told me that Morrison is believed to have been a white man.

wanted to live with the Chickasaws, who had once invited them to settle in their territory. The Chickasaw Council, however, never reached a decision to accept them. In 1854 a federal act appropriating a $5,000 grant to settle the Catawbas west of the Mississippi River was approved, but the grant later seems to have reverted to the surplus fund of the United States Treasury. In the meantime most of the Catawbas moved away from Cherokee, some going to live with the Choctaws and others returning to South Carolina.[13] By 1852 there were only about a dozen Catawbas living at Cherokee. In 1890 there were only two at Cherokee: the widow of a Cherokee man and her daughter (Covington 1954).

In 1856 the geologist Oscar M. Lieber (1858:327-342) estimated that there were 50 Catawbas living in South Carolina. In collecting a vocabulary of the Catawba language, Lieber said that his informant, who was working for him as a camp servant, knew that he did not speak the Catawba language as well as his parents spoke it; still, children did not begin to learn English until they were 10 or 12 years old.

Thus, in the first half of the nineteenth century the economy of South Carolina became dependent upon one-crop agriculture—cotton. As a consequence, outside pressure on the Catawbas became greater because their reservation included land that could be used in the production of cotton. Through a series of pressures, some of which were of questionable legality, the Catawbas were eventually pushed onto a small tract of land that is today known as the Old Reservation.[14] As the Civil War approached, the Catawbas were an obscure enclave in a social system that was beginning to break down. The South became more and more defensive as it expended great effort in justifying the God-given rightness

---

13. In 1850 there were 110 Catawbas: 20 men, 43 women, 20 male children under ten years of age, and 27 female children under ten years of age. Of these, 76 were in North Carolina, and the remainder were in South Carolina, some of the latter living on a farm that was in "public property" (Covington 1954:46).

14. The Old Reservation contains approximately 630 acres. It is situated on the west bank of the Catawba River on or near the site of Newtown, the principal Catawba village in the latter part of the eighteenth century.

of its plural social order. When the Civil War came, a few Catawbas served in the Confederate Army, thus indicating their agreement with white ideology.

In the decades preceding the Civil War, outside pressure forced the Catawbas onto a fraction of their original reservation. With the foundations of their former social position destroyed, they struggled to find a place for themselves. They were members of a plural society that was theoretically stable, but was actually troubled by many internal conflicts and contradictions. The struggle of the Catawbas continued after the Civil War ended, but it took place in a somewhat different setting. The Civil War destroyed the legal structure of the old plural order, while leaving South Carolina with the problem of economic and political re-organization. After a period of profound instability, South Carolina eventually assumed something of its old plural order backed by a racist ideology. White men were supposed to remain white and black men were supposed to remain black; no one quite knew what to do with mestizos, particularly those who refused to be treated as Negroes. Consequently, the Catawbas were faced with a crisis in identity. Since they had insufficient land, they were forced to become acculturated in order to make a living; at the same time, as they lost their culture they ran the risk of being regarded as mestizos. They were faced with a dilemma: were they to be a race or a nation?

As we have seen, ante-bellum South Carolina specialized in a cotton economy. Slavery seems to have been on its way out near the end of the eighteenth century, but the introduction of cotton gave it a new impetus. This re-emphasis on slavery cannot be explained in terms of efficiency; if anything slaves were less efficient than free laborers. Slavery was re-emphasized because there were few free laborers available at a time when cotton planters needed a large, disciplined labor force and because the ownership of slaves conferred social prestige (Tang 1958:30-31). Through this one-crop economy and slave labor, Southern agriculture became inflexible. Slave labor was so specialized in the production of cotton, it became virtually impossible to divert it to any other enterprise. "It appears that Southern planters, after having invented slavery for the sake of cotton, later found themselves forced to grow cotton for the sake of its slaves" (Tang 1958:32). Southern society was full of basic contradictions; as these contradictions became more apparent, the white minority became increasingly defensive, eventually becoming embroiled in the Civil War.

After the slaves were emancipated the greatest economic problems in the post-war South were to establish a relationship between landless people and land owners and to establish a relationship between penniless farmers and capitalists. The first problem was "solved" by the crop-share system and the second by the crop-lien system. In the crop-share system a landowner provided his share-croppers with work animals and equipment, part of the necessary seed and fertilizers, and, in some cases, credit. After the crop was sold, the proceeds were divided between the share-croppers and the landowner. The landowner, of course, had considerable power, including the right to decide what crops would be grown and how his land would be used.

After the Civil War had depleted the wealth of the planters, most of whose investment was in slaves, the local storekeeper was the only one to whom one could turn for credit. In the crop-lien system, a farmer got credit from a particular storekeeper in the form of food, clothing, implements, and so forth. The storekeeper got from 20 to 100 percent more profit from this merchandise than he got from cash purchases. He protected his interests by taking out a mortgage on the crops of his credit customers. Thus the local storekeeper became a powerful man in the economy. He gave credit, sold supplies, and bought cotton. In many cases, those who obtained credit in this way became virtual peons. Until they paid off their debts in full, they were under the control of the storekeeper. No other merchant or storekeeper would give them credit until their debts were paid (Tang 1958:37-44).

These institutions of crop-share and crop-lien gave landowners and storekeepers an inordinate amount of power over farmers and share-croppers; on the positive side, however, the crop-share system enabled landless people to use land, and the crop-lien system made it possible for poor people to get credit. They were transitional measures that made it possible for the South to resume agricultural production. The long-term effects of these institutions, however, were less desirable. Both were self-perpetuating systems which led the South again into the "strait-jacket of cotton" (Tang 1958). The South became what economists now call an underdeveloped society.

Post-war South Carolina faced political and social problems that were even more serious than her economic problems. In 1865 the President of the United States appointed a governor of South Carolina, directing him to enroll eligible voters and hold a constitutional convention. The most outstanding legislation of this convention was the "Black Code," a series of statutes designed to regulate racial relationships. This code defined a Negro as a person having one-eighth or more Negro blood; and for the first time in the history of South Carolina, marriage between Negroes and whites was formally declared illegal and existing marriages were declared null. In addition, there were a number of additional restrictions on the freedom of Negroes. Although slavery no longer existed, the ideological assumptions that supported it remained: South Carolinians believed that Negroes could neither be trusted to work nor to obey the law without special restraints (Wallace 1951:566-567).

The federal government responded by vetoing the "Black Code" in 1866; somewhat vindictively they attempted to give Negroes a political status equal to whites. Subsequently the South was occupied by federal troops and placed under martial law in an effort to protect the rights of the Negroes. In 1868 there was another constitutional convention; unlike the all-white convention of 1866, representatives in this convention consisted of 48 whites and 76 Negroes. The constitution it framed allowed interracial marriage and requested that there be no racial bias in publicly supported schools and colleges.

The whites, however, were determined to keep their monopoly on power. In 1868-70, the Ku Klux Klan was organized as a secret organization whose primary purpose was to terrorize Negroes. York County, in which the Catawba Old Reservation is situated, seems to have been the area of

greatest Klan activity in South Carolina. Gradually through
a variety of means the whites regained their monopoly on
power. In 1879 South Carolina again passed a law making
interracial marriage illegal; this time it forbade marriages
between whites and Indians as well as between whites and
Negroes (Wallace 1951:569-590, 632).[15]

In retrospect, it is difficult to see how the marriage law
of 1879 could have been framed with reference to the
Catawbas, who at that time numbered barely a hundred. A
more likely explanation is that it was designed to regulate
certain enclaves of Indian-Negro-white mestizos. These
mestizos are scattered throughout the eastern United States,
but they are most heavily concentrated in the low country of
North and South Carolina (Gilbert 1946, 1949; Berry 1945,
1963). When first "discovered," these enclaves were generally situated in inaccessible areas: swamps, pine barrens, and
tidewater islands and peninsulas (Gilbert 1946:438). The
isolation of these people began to break down during and
after the Civil War, and this trend accelerated as roads and
means of communication were improved.

The mestizos of North and South Carolina are known by
different names in different places, and they differ in other
respects as well. Consequently, it is difficult to make gen-
eralizations about them, but the following statements seem
to hold for most of them. (1) Before the Civil War, after
which most of them were discovered, they existed "outside"
of society in inaccessible locations (Berry 1945:35). (2)
Most of them claimed some degree of Indian ancestry, but
they could not satisfactorily trace descent from nominate
Indian societies. (3) When first discovered, they shared the
culture of poor whites with little or no trace of aboriginal
culture (Gilbert 1948:428). (4) After being discovered, they
had to deal with whites who conceived of others as being
either white, Indian, or Negro, with virtually nothing in
between. (5) Most of them refused to be categorized as
Negroes, while the whites were in most cases reluctant to

---

15. A third constitution was framed in 1895, sanctioning the marriage
laws of 1865 and 1879; in addition, racial segregation was enforced in the
schools.

accept them as equals. Consequently they occupied a social position that was extremely ambiguous (Berry 1948:36-37).

In this social background the Catawbas were forced into an identity crisis. The Old Reservation consisted of less than 700 acres, only a few of which could be cultivated. Therefore, they were faced with two unattractive alternatives. They could stay on the Old Reservation, retaining their Indian identity and remaining nominally a nation, the outcome of which would have meant starvation. On the other hand, they could go off the reservation and share-crop; however, this would require acculturation, a process whereby the Catawbas risked joining the ambiguous social status of mestizos.

What they did was to combine the two alternatives. When Albert Gatschet (1900:527) visited the Old Reservation in 1881, he found that about 85 Catawbas were living on the Reservation while about 40 were farming in Mecklenburg County, North Carolina.[16] When Scaife (1896) visited the Reservation in 1893-96, he too found that the Catawbas would go out to share-crop for a year or two and then return to the Reservation. However, even though share-cropping helped, they were extremely poor. Scaife's impression was that the Catawba standard of living was "a little below the standard of the average Southern Negro." They lived in small, crudely built log huts that reminded him of "the typical Negro home in the farming regions of the South." In warm weather they cooked outside over an open fire. The only domestic animals he saw were a cow and two mules. Some of the Catawbas were forced to beg on the streets of Rock Hill.

The Catawbas could not, of course, obtain credit unless they were share-croppers. I suspect that few of them became share-croppers because they were frequently cheated out of their earnings by land-owners. Several of my informants told of their parents "making a crop," only to be thrown off the land before the crop was harvested. This could have been rationalized by the landowners in a variety of ways. The Indians were supposed to be indolent, deceitful, and thievish; and after all, they could go back to the reservation.

16. Gatschet mistakenly says they were in Muhlenberg County. He estimates that about one-third of them could speak the Catawba language.

In spite of becoming increasingly acculturated and
genetically mixed with whites, the Catawbas managed to retain an unambiguous status as Indians.[17] They accomplished
this by several means. For one thing, they expressed a strong
antipathy for Negroes, who in turn were supposed to be
afraid of Indians: "it is said that a negro cannot be induced
to go on the Indian's land" (Scaife 1896).[18]

Another means of keeping their Indian identity was by
making and selling Indian objects. Although the Catawbas
had been using guns for about 200 years, at the end of the
nineteenth century some of the old men made bows and
arrows for sale. A more important source of income was
the manufacture of pottery. This was made by traditional
techniques, but the objects were mostly modern in form:
pipes "in the form of squirrels, turtles, birds, pots, shoes, and
other familiar objects," and "graceful pitchers, flower-jugs,
vases, and various kinds of toys and ornaments" (Scaife
1898:19).

The making and selling of pottery was particularly important; unlikely as it seems, it was one of their most reliable
sources of income. We recall that Smyth mentioned the sale
of pottery in the late eighteenth century, and that Simms
mentioned it in the early nineteenth century. This pottery
was usually made by a woman with the assistance of her
children. It was carried to Rock Hill and surrounding areas
where it was either sold or bartered for old clothes and other
necessities (Scaife 1898:19). One informant told me that
her mother used to trade pots to storekeepers for the
measures they could contain of corn-meal and flour.

Another Indian way of making money was to dress up
in Indian costumes for appearances at events involving entertainment or recreation. The Catawbas used to attend state
fairs and similar events dressed as Indians. A few were professional Indians. One for example, worked as an Indian in
circuses and medicine shows.

---

17. Scaife says that in 1893-96, of the 80 on the reservation "less than
a dozen were of pure Indian blood, the remainder being half-breeds or
more nearly white" (1896:18).

18. This belief has been extraordinarily durable. While doing field
work I was told that a Negro will not go on Indian land at night.

In addition to these various ways of keeping their image as Indians while earning income, the Catawbas maintained a council, an internal political structure. Apparently, the structure of this council became more formalized as the Catawbas won increasing recognition and support from South Carolina. In the closing decades of the nineteenth century, when the Catawbas were given an $800 annuity from the state, they often were without a chief (Speck and Schaeffer 1942:565). However, in the 1930's when $9,500 per annum was appropriated for the Catawbas, the council consisted of five men.[19] These were a chief, a committee chairman, two councilmen, and a secretary.

The chief of the Catawbas was their representative to the outside world. He was a man who could speak the Catawba language, or a reasonable facsimile of the language, and who could play the role that whites expected an Indian to play. There is some disagreement about the scope of his power in the council. Speck says that he held the deciding vote, while my information suggests that the committee chairman was the most powerful (Speck 1942:566). One of my Catawba informants put it this way:

A long time ago, outsiders used to believe that whatever the chief said went; but that was not so. That was why they had the committee. If a person had land in cultivation, he could sell the right to another person. He cleared it up. It was a written agreement. Three of the five on the committee had to sign it. The main one to sign was the chairman. If he refused, then a meeting of the whole committee would have to be called.

The main duties of the council were to handle appropriations and to settle internal disputes. They were guided by custom in these matters. For example, one was not permitted to build a house within 300 yards of another house; this allowed space for a garden and for firewood. If a decision could not be reached in a dispute, it was taken before a magistrate.

---

19. Coming from the Office of the Secretary of State of South Carolina, this money was spent in the following way: (1) The Indian agent received $500; (2) the doctor who administered to the Catawbas was then paid for services rendered; (3) next came burial expenses for all funerals; (4) then came educational expenses, including books and a teacher's salary; (5) and the remainder was equally divided among Catawbas who were listed on a tribal roll that was drawn up every April.

The information I collected suggests that the man who
played the role of chief was above all a man who could
represent the Catawbas as Indians. When curious whites came
to visit the reservation they were directed to see him. How
could there be Indians without a chief? And how could a
man be chief without speaking the language and knowing
"Indian lore"? The last traditional chief was a man of considerable ability. When he went into Rock Hill, he always
wore his Indian costume, one important article being a Plains
Indian war bonnet. In this attire, he visited the State Legislature every year to make a plea for more assistance to the
Catawbas. His argument was that the whites should help
the Catawbas in payment for the help the Catawbas gave
the white settlers in colonial times.

Until well into the twentieth century, Catawba men did
not have a secure place in the economy. A few of them farmed
the meager land that was available on the reservation. In
winter some of them cut cord wood and sold it to whites
for fuel and to the textile mills to fire their boilers. It sold
for eight to ten dollars per wagon load. Many people, both
white and Catawba, told me that this used to be the primary
occupation of Catawba men. If true it was primary in the
sense of being about the only occupation open to them.
It could not have been very profitable. It so happens that
the man who sold most of this cord wood was the last
traditional chief. He took it into Rock Hill in a wagon pulled
by mules; on these occasions he always dressed in his war
bonnet and costume. Thus the sale of cord wood was probably
more conspicuous than important.

A few Catawba men worked on farms for wages, but
they generally went out of the vicinity of Rock Hill to do
this. A few landowners in the Rock Hill area would hire
Catawbas to work in cotton, but in general they hired only
women. The whites regarded the Catawba men as good hunters
and fishermen but as poor farmers. According to the whites,
this was partly due to ignorance of farming techniques. In
addition the whites believed that Catawba men were unwilling to do the labor necessary in dawn-to-dusk farming.
One white man told me the following story:

The Indians used to bother me about working on my farm. One time I hired one to come help me plow. I hitched up before dawn and started, but he didn't show up until seven o'clock. He was a big, husky one. He worked about an hour and said he had a toothache. After that, I never hired another one.

At the same time, the whites seem to have been perfectly willing to hire Catawba women to work in the fields. One old woman told me about working on her father's farm and about working for a white man near Rock Hill:

I would hoe and pick cotton for wages. A bunch of us women would go and work for a man up near town. Young girls, mothers, and grandmothers. We got paid at the end of every week. The men wouldn't go out much. They weren't on public works at that time.

As a supplementary source of food, the Catawbas hunted, fished, and gathered wild food. Fishing seems to have been the most important of these means of exploiting natural food supplies. Among the fishing devices they used were nets, trotlines, and set hooks. A trotline is a line strung across a river or stream with a series of baited hooks attached to it by short lines; once or twice a day a fisherman would traverse the trotline in a boat, removing fish and rebaiting the hooks. A set-hook was a six-foot cane pole attached to a three-foot line and a baited hook. These were stuck in the bank and checked once or twice a day. The Catawbas caught mostly catfish and "red horses," the latter being a carp-like fish.

Both men and women gathered wild fruits and vegetables. The more important fruits and vegetables were huckleberries, wild plums, poke greens, dandelion greens, and wild onions. Their beverages were sassafras tea, blackberry wine, and home-brewed beer. They also made a beverage by mixing the pod of the honey locust tree with broom straw or pine needles.

In addition to earning money by working in white-owned cotton fields, Catawba women continued to manufacture and sell pottery.

When I was growing up it was a necessity to make pottery. That's the way we got our clothes and part of our groceries.

There was never any farming to amount to anything. In the last few years they have started gardening. When I was growing up we had corn, but I don't remember any gardens. There were eight of us children. We didn't play; we just worked in clay— that was our living. I can remember three or four families getting clay across the river at one time. Most of my mother's pottery was taken to the mountains for sale—to Cherokee. They got it for almost nothing.

While some men made a few pieces of small pottery, women made the great majority of it.

Although my informant did not remember kitchen gardens, they were in fact grown and most of the work was done by women. A man would plow the garden and prepare it for planting. After that a woman did most of the remaining work with the assistance of her children. None of the produce was sold, but a family would often share their surplus with needy families. Some of the vegetables were canned for use during the winter.

Women were definitely pivotal in the household economy. Consequently, there is a strong suggestion that the family structure was matrifocal. Unable to rely on a single man for steady income (because there was no way for him to earn one), a woman often had relationships with several men in succession. In the latter part of the nineteenth century, when a woman gave birth to a child by a white man the child was given the surname of his father, "so they would know not to marry back into his family." Thus, it was possible for a woman to have children with different surnames. Later it became the custom for a woman to give her illegitimate children her own surname. One of my informants told me that before 1910 Indian status could only be obtained through having an Indian mother. Thus, the children of a white man and a Catawba mother would be included on the tribal roll; the children of an Indian man and a white woman would not.

A woman was most reliant on her husband in the early years of their marriage; however, even then she could appeal to her relatives for aid. Later, when her children were older she could rely on them for some income. I was told of one case where a mother hired out her son when he was 12 years old. This was called "working for wages." He lived and worked with a white farm family for a year. In compensation, he was given room and board, and at the end of the year he was paid a sum in cash, which he subsequently turned over to his mother.

Even though the Catawbas had several means of maintaining a semblance of Indian identity, in the late 1800's and early 1900's they were steadily losing their culture. In 1900 less than a dozen Catawbas could speak the language. As a means of increasing their separateness from non-Indians, while at the same time realizing other advantages, the Catawbas made a bold decision: they became Mormon converts.

As early as 1773, the Catawbas requested that a Christian missionary be sent to them, but none was sent (Alden 1944:304, 353). Later they attended several of the churches built by whites near the Old Reservation, but never in great numbers. However, when the first Mormon elders arrived, the Catawbas were greatly interested.

Founded in 1830 by Joseph Smith, the Mormon religion is the only major religion that gives American Indians a place in their scriptures. According to *The Book of Mormon*, a group of Jerusalem Israelites came to the New World around 600 B. C. Subsequently, they split into two antagonistic factions: the Nephites, who were generally in God's favor; and the Lamanites, who became degenerate pagans cursed with having a dark skin. In the fourth century A.D., the Lamanites succeeded in killing all the Nephites in a great battle at the hill of Cumorah in New York State. The descendants of the victorious Lamanites are the American Indians, who at the time of first European contact are believed to have been nomadic, non-agricultural, and degenerate.

However, *The Book of Mormon* contains a prophesy that these Lamanites will be brought back into the fold, whereupon they will become "a white and delightsome people" (1950:2; Nephi 30:6). From the first, the Mormons were dedicated to reconverting the Indians. However, they were prevented from doing this in the western United States because it antagonized the whites (O'Dea 1957). In the southern United States, they also met resistance, but of a different sort. The Mormons were a "peculiar people," suffering persecution from the outset of their movement. In the 1870's organizations of gentile ladies (as the Mormons called them) all over the United States denounced the "Asiatic church," sending missionaries to Utah to convert them to other religions. The Federal government began exerting considerable pressure on the Mormons in the 1880's to cease the practice of polygamy. All of this was widely publicized in the newspaper and in church literature. In the South suspicion towards these peculiar people was compounded by the bitter feelings that remained from the Civil War and Reconstruction; outsiders were not welcome.

Under these circumstances, elders Charles E. Robinson and H. Miller first made contact with the Catawbas in May 1883. The first meetings were apparently held in Fort Mill, South Carolina, some five miles from the Old Reservation. The Catawbas were clearly interested in becoming converts. The attitude of the whites, however, the Mormons found to be quite different: "We find it the hardest to get a place to stop overnight. We find the ministers the worst of all, for they have an influence over the people. One preached last Sunday openly that we ought to be mobbed out of the country."[20] In September of the same year, elder Robinson died of "chills, fever, and yellow jaundice."[21]

Shortly afterwards, elder Miller was joined by elder Joseph Willey, who had just returned from having made first Mormon contact with the Cherokees. Willey had no success with the Cherokees because only a few could speak English, and "the Baptists, Methodists and Quakers had made it their business to tell them we were bad men." The Catawbas were different. "They all talk the English language . . . and are healthy, industrious and law-abiding citizens." On November 11, 1883, elders Willey and Miller baptized the first 5 Catawbas. Subsequently Willey and a new elder, whose surname was Humphrey, baptized 17 Catawbas and 4 whites; they also organized a Sunday school. In May 1884 Willey

20. *History of Southern States Mission,* Library of the Church of Jesus Christ of Latter Day Saints, Salt Lake City, Utah. Entry for June 9, 1883, quoting the *Bear Lake Democrat.*
21. *Deseret Evening News,* Salt Lake City, Utah, October 3, 1883.

tells of "holding meetings every Sunday, talking by the fire-side every night, and have the promise of a coat of tar and feathers."[22]

Apparently elders Willey and Humphrey were forced to leave. Later in the month their replacements, elders Franklin A. Fraughton and Wiley G. Cragun, were mobbed by whites while on the reservation (Jenson 1941:121-122). Fraughton was caught and horse-whipped; Cragun escaped into the woods under a hail of gunfire, suffering a slight flesh wound in his chin. Later the whites threatened to kill the next elder they caught, but the elders continued to go to the reservation and hold meetings even though they sometimes had to hide "while a crowd of drunken men caroused around in the Nation making the night hideous by their whooping and yelling."[23] Hampered in not being able to visit the reservation openly, the elders organized a Sunday school with "one of the Lamanite brethren to superintend it."[24]

One motive of the Catawba converts to Mormonism was to emigrate West. The dominant themes in nineteenth century Mormonism were association of the church with land (Zion, i.e., Utah, Colorado, etc.), separatism from civilization (i.e., the United States), and the gathering of the faithful in Zion (O'Dea 1957). In February 1887 eight Catawbas emigrated to Colorado, "and the rest would gladly follow their example, had they the necessary means."[25] Apparently few additional Catawbas emigrated, but the elders persuaded some to move near Spartanburg, South Carolina, where Mormons were more tolerantly received.[26] Those remaining on the reservation appear to have worshipped secretly. Scaife, for example, says that in 1893-96 there was "neither a church

22. *Ibid.*, May 20, 1884.
23. *Ibid.*, March 31, 1887.
24. *Ibid.*, May 17, 1887.
25. *Ibid.*, March 31, 1887. In January 1896 the Office of Indian Affairs received a petition signed by P. H. Head, a leader, and twenty-five additional Catawbas, embracing six families living near Sanford, Colorado. They requested permission to settle among the Utes on the Uintah Reservation in Utah. They did not succeed in this, possibly because the government policy of the time was to abolish all relations with Indians (Anonymous 1897:11).
26. *Ibid.*, May 17, 1887.

nor a school on the reservation—it is a shame that in a Christian country they never hear the Gospel preached. In our ardor for foreign missions let us not pass by and neglect the heathen in our midst" (Scaife 1896:22).

Regardless of the dominant motives of the first Catawbas to join the Mormon church, their identification with the church was a source of alternative values. At a time when they were becoming physically and culturally like whites, it both set them apart from whites, mestizos, and Negroes and made them feel that they were in some sense a chosen people. It was a source of self-esteem. The first elders, for example, felt that the whites did not want the Catawbas to become Mormons because it might interfere with their having sexual relations with Catawba women.

The majority of them [the Catawbas] have embraced the Gospel, but it is hard, under the influence of so-called civilization, to get all of them to refrain from the evil habits which had such a hold upon them when the Gospel found them. When the Elders went in among them, the neighboring whites had, in "The Nation," as they call it, a regular place of resort for lewd purposes. As soon as the principles of the Gospel were taught them, and they were made to sense their condition they ceased their evil practices and accepted the truth.[27]

Both the Mormons and the Catawbas thought of themselves as being in conflict with "so-called civilization"; they embraced a religion that both made this conflict explicit and provided a source of self-esteem.

---

27. *Ibid., loc. cit.*

CHAPTER V

Assimilation in a Changing Society

In 1900 the town of Fort Mill, a small community situated a few miles north of Rock Hill, celebrated the beginning of a new millennium. To commemorate the event the townspeople erected several stone monuments, each containing a series of inscriptions. I visited these monuments, and when I read the inscriptions I thought it curious that they were oriented toward the past instead of toward the future. The inscriptions confirm, as it were, the existence of three kinds of people: whites, Negroes, and Indians. The whites are depicted as the dominant people, the people who settled the country and civilized it with Christianity and agriculture. The Negroes are depicted as descendants of slaves who did not really want the freedom that came after the Civil War, and as friends of paternalistic whites. The Catawbas are depicted as the "remnant" of a once powerful warlike nation who were "ever friends of the white settlers," having aided them both in the Revolution and in the Civil War; shorn of their former glory, the Catawbas lived as wards of the state. Reading these inscriptions, I felt that the people who erected the monuments thought that things would never change.

Actually, by 1900 change had already begun. We have already seen that Fort Mill was the place where the Mormon elders first made contact with the Catawbas. In addition, a more sweeping source of change was present—industry. In 1881 the first textile mill in the vicinity of Rock Hill opened its doors, and by 1900 the number of mills had increased to half a dozen (Brown 1953:186, 273). After a hydroelectric dam was built on the Catawba River in 1904, Rock Hill rapidly developed into one of the industrial centers of the southern

81

piedmont (Brown 1953:-244). Between 1900 and 1940, the total value added by manufacture in the southern piedmont increased from $11,846,196 to $105,322,861, a relative growth of 789 per cent (Tang 1958:66).

However, even though industrialization was underway, the South did not enjoy true economic development until the late 1930's and early 1940's, the era of the New Deal and wartime prosperity. In 1929, for example, agriculture supplied approximately 26 percent of the South's "earned" income; in 1961 it supplied less than 9 percent. A more vivid index of economic development is that there are 1,400,000 fewer tenant farmers today than there were in 1935 (Goldschmidt 1963:229-230).

In the early decades of this century, the Catawbas continued to live pretty much as they did in the closing decades of the last century. In addition to farming and cutting cord wood, some of the Catawbas continued in occupations that were either associated with Indians or peculiar in other respects. One man, for example, was an expert with high-powered rifles; for awhile he was employed by the Winchester Company demonstrating their rifles. One of his favorite demonstrations was to shoot at a blank target, outlining an Indian head with bullet holes. He also worked briefly for a local automobile dealer who sold Pontiacs.

Apparently, the first Catawba to earn regular wages for non-agricultural work was a man who began operating a ferry across the Catawba River in 1916. The following year the Catawba River flooded and washed out the bridge on the road between Rock Hill and Charlotte, North Carolina. While the bridge was being rebuilt another Catawba, who was at that time the chief, operated a second ferry. The second ferry was temporary, but the man who operated the first ferry was succeeded by his son who continued to operate it for over 30 years. Toward the end of his service, several articles about him appeared in local newspapers, their theme being that he had faithfully served the whites just as the Catawbas of old had served the first colonists. Thus, while operating a ferry was not an "Indian" occupation, it was nonetheless a peculiar occupation.

So long as the structure of the larger society remained

the same, the scope of Catawba social change was necessarily restricted. As we have seen, the sociocultural sections in a plural society are kept distinct by formidable social barriers which are maintained by powerful internal pressures. These social barriers and pressures did not appreciably weaken until industrialization and economic development accelerated, at which time the plural character of South Carolina society lessened, and the Catawbas began to experience a new kind of social change—assimilation. Through a series of informal decisions by particular individuals a few Catawbas began to realize privileges that had previously been limited to whites. The three main avenues of assimilation were employment in industry, education, and intermarriage with whites.

The first Catawba to be employed in industry was hired in 1918. He had been working on a farm for a man who was also a superintendent in a textile mill. Not only did the superintendent set a precedent by hiring a Catawba to do mill work, according to some reports he also accepted him into his home in Rock Hill as a boarder. Being perhaps the first Catawba to be clearly in competition with whites, he encountered initial resentment and hostility stemming from a basic contradiction in the social position of the Catawbas.

When he started, they said, "Who is going to learn this Indian to work?" The superintendent said, "We all are." They didn't want to teach him because he was an Indian.

We had a lot of trouble with the whites at first. They didn't want the Indians to work because the state furnished money for us — our houses and doctor bills. They didn't want our kids to go to white schools. They would try to block us from going in the mills.

This was a beginning for the Catawbas, but few additional Catawbas were hired by the mills until the late 1930's and early 1940's. Like the landowners who hired Catawbas to work in the cotton fields, the mills initially seem to have hired more women than men.

Paradoxically, the religion that at first set the Catawbas apart from other people later became an important medium of assimilation. This was particularly true in education, where the Mormon religion benefited the Catawbas both directly and indirectly. A direct benefit was that the Mormons believe that man has an infinite capacity for improvement; accordingly, they place high value on free will, rationality, self-improvement, and education (O'Dea 1957:126-133, 143-154). Mormon teachings instilled a desire for education in the Catawbas, but their aspirations were at first blocked locally because the whites would not allow them to attend public schools. A few of them took advantage of the alternatives that were available. Five or six of them went to the Indian School at Carlisle, Pennsylvania, and a few went to the school at the Cherokee reservation.

The Catawbas used voluntary labor to erect a school building of their own in 1897-98.[1] At first they seem to have been unable to find a teacher, but eventually this need was met through one of the indirect effects of Mormonism. After it became clear that the Catawbas were seriously interested in Mormonism, other religious groups became interested in their spiritual welfare. Several Protestant churches began sending in missionaries to try to win Catawba converts. One consequence of this was that the first teachers among the Catawbas were a Presbyterian man and his wife. They taught regular classes in the day school and attempted to convert the Catawbas to Presbyterianism on Sundays. Few Catawbas became Presbyterian converts, but several of them attended the day school with considerable enthusiasm. Many of the first students were adults. My informants told me about one man who spoke no English until he was eighteen; but once the school was available he attended regularly, and even when he was in his forties he occasionally attended.

After the Presbyterian couple discontinued their work because of their failure to win converts, the school was occasionally taught by Mormon missionaries.[2] In the absence

---

1. In 1899-1900 the Catawbas used voluntary labor to build their first church. A second church was built in 1928. Unfortunately this second church was built on the pattern of flat-roofed Mormon churches in the Western United States. It eventually developed leaks and rotted. Construction on their third church began in 1950. The second and third churches, like the first, were built using voluntary labor.

2. The Catawbas requested a Mormon missionary to teach Sunday school and day school as early as 1908. At that time, about 85 percent of the Catawbas were members of the church, and "the rest were believers." *Journal History*, Library of the Church of Jesus Christ of Latter-day Saints, Salt Lake City, Utah, 1908, July 29, p. 5.

of a teacher from outside, one of the Catawbas who had become literate taught school. Eventually, South Carolina provided annual funds for a professional school teacher. For many years the education of the Catawbas ended with the elementary school on the reservation; they were not allowed to attended the all-white high school in Rock Hill.

Like mill work, Catawba education was at first a change of limited scope; neither mill work nor education appreciably altered the internal structure of Catawba society nor their position in the larger society. Thus, in the early 1930's most of the Catawbas continued to be employed in small-scale farming, cutting cord wood, hunting and fishing, and various "peculiar" occupations. The only differences were that they were getting an elementary education, and a few of them were working in textile mills. But in most respects, they continued to live as they had. The chief, for example, continued visiting the legislature every year to plead for more state assistance to the Catawbas.

In the late 1930's and early 1940's, however, two things accelerated social change among the Catawbas: the New Deal and the labor demand in World War II. When Catawbas were asked when the greatest change occurred in their way of life, their unanimous answer was 1940 to 1943. This was when many Catawba men worked for the W.P.A. and when both men and women started working in the textile mills in large numbers. At this time, farming had steadily been declining for several years. Members of the younger generation began basing their aspirations on "public works." One Catawba said this: "Farming started going out in 1935, during the hard times. That was when Hoover was in. Most of the Indians worked on the W.P.A. Some few of them worked in textiles before the W.P.A. The W.P.A. was the first big public works that they were on."[3]

Employment by the W.P.A. marked the first general acceptance of the Catawbas in public works, but the Catawbas attribute their progress to mill work. Another Catawba said: "About the time I was born, they couldn't work in the plants.

---

3. The Catawbas regularly refer to themselves as "they" instead of "we" when talking about their recent history. We will consider the implications of this usage in the next chapter.

Some of them started in World War I, but most of them started in World War II. Work in the mills improved them. When people are held down and then get a chance to work, they will improve. Since 1943 they have built up tremendously. Before that, they had no electric lights or water pumps. There was only one well on the whole reservation." While they were winning acceptance as disciplined, responsible workers, they began to win acceptance in other ways.

At the same time the Catawbas began to be employed in large numbers by the W.P.A. and the textile mills, their children began to attend the Rock Hill High School. According to the laws of South Carolina, this was illegal. They were admitted into the high school the same way they were first admitted into the mills; a single white man, the superintendent of the school, had the courage to ignore tradition and admit them. Around a half dozen began attending high school between 1935 and 1940. They were not, however, allowed to ride the school buses; they caught rides with Catawbas who commuted each day to work in the mills.

From the time the first Catawba started working in the textile mills until the early 1940's, the Catawbas broke one social barrier after another, gradually and without ostentation. In the words of one of my Catawba informants:

There was trouble at first. They [the whites] didn't want the Indians as competitors. But they kept it up. They didn't go about it in an overbearing way. Between 1925 and 1930 they couldn't eat at certain places. The whites have changed a lot, but there are still a few that won't associate.

By the 1940's, the Catawbas were fully committed to employment in the textile mills. There could be no turning back.

Even though the Catawbas were at last becoming assimilated, they doggedly continued visiting the legislature every year to plead for more assistance from the state. Finally, in 1941 South Carolina appointed a committee to negotiate with the Office of Indian Affairs and the Federal Farm Security Administration for the purpose of giving aid to the Catawbas. After several conferences the Federal agencies agreed to "rehabilitate" the Catawbas, but the proceedings were interrupted by the onset of World War II (Bradford 1944).

In March 1943 the Office of Indian Affairs reopened negotiations, and South Carolina appointed another committee. Later in the year a "Memorandum of Understanding" was signed by the State of South Carolina, the Catawbas, and the Office of Indian Affairs. In this Memorandum, South Carolina agreed to allocate $75,000 for the purchase of additional tax-exempt lands; if any of this money remained after the purchase of lands, it was to be turned over to the Office of Indian Affairs. This land, along with the Old Reservation, was to be given to the Office of Indian Affairs to be held in trust.[4] In addition, South Carolina gave assurance that the Catawbas would be made citizens of South Carolina and that they would be allowed to attend public schools, high schools, and institutions of higher learning.

Officials from the Office of Indian Affairs agreed to appropriate annual funds for the Catawbas under the Johnson-O'Malley Act. They also agreed to provide trained people to assist the Catawbas in developing arts and crafts and to make loans and grants for their economic development. In addition, they agreed to provide general medical treatment as well as the use of Indian Service hospitals for serious psychiatric and physical illnesses.

In February 1944 the committee submitted its report to the House and Senate of South Carolina. The members of the committee reported having purchased 3,482.8 acres of land at a total cost of $70,132.50, an average of $20.43 per acre.[5] This land was selected by the committee in consultation with the Office of Indian Affairs. In the spring of 1944, some of the Catawbas began to move on the "New Reservation" under the supervision of the Office of Indian Affairs.

The ostensible motive of South Carolina in this transaction was to repay the Catawbas "for patriotic service their forefathers had rendered and the financial obligations like-

---

4. The Office of Indian Affairs did not, however, accept responsibility for the Old Reservation; it continues to be held in trust by South Carolina.

5. This land was purchased in several tracts, some of which were not contiguous with the Old Reservation or with each other. They were named the Friedham tract, Springstein tract, Catoe-Fewell tract, Spencer tract, and Dabney-Ratteree tract.

wise due them because of the unscrupulous methods employed by white citizens in business transactions with them especially in acquiring title to most of their lands." However, a more practical motive can be seen in the following passage:

In the last half century tax money running into hundreds of thousands of dollars has been appropriated from the State Treasury for the maintenance of the Catawbas, and that would seem another potent reason why South Carolinians should be interested in the Indians (Bradford 1944:13).

For South Carolina, this was an opportunity to allow the Federal Government to assume responsibility for the Catawbas. For the Catawbas, the New Reservation was a mixed blessing. It was an advantage in that it gave them room for improvement; the drawback was that most of the Federal aid they were promised was conditioned upon their practicing agriculture.

In upper South Carolina in recent years thousands of white people have moved from the farms into towns to seek other ways of making a living. Will the Indians follow the example the whites have thus set them, or will they settle permanently on the land the State has bought for them and cooperate with the Federal authorities in the effort that will be made to help them to independence as farmers? If the answer should be in the negative in response to the latter prong of the question, a regrettable situation will be brought about. Thence on, neither the State nor Federal Government would likely look favorably upon any suggestion of further aid for the Catawbas (Bradford 1944:29-30).

With respect to Catawba history, the acquisition of the New Reservation was an ironic afterthought. At the very time the Catawbas were increasingly being assimilated into an industrial society, they were given land which they were expected to farm.

In addition to assimilation through education and industrial employment, the Catawbas were also being assimilated through intermarriage with whites. Under South Carolina miscegenation laws, marriages between Indians and whites were illegal. In spite of this, however, a few Catawbas married whites in the early 1900's. As was the case in industrial employment and education, the Catawbas were able to marry whites as a results of the decisions of particular individuals; when a Catawba decided to marry a white, he knew of one or two officials in the state who would perform the ceremony. In the 1940's the frequency of Catawba-white intermarriage increased sharply, many of the married couples subsequently moving into Rock Hill to live. I spoke to one woman who even cautioned her children not to marry a Cherokee, "because you never know what you are marrying into" (i.e., they could be distant kin). At the time I did field work, I estimate that well over 75 percent of the people on the Catawba tribal roll were judged to be white by local people.

As the Catawbas became increasingly assimilated into the larger society, they acquired new values and expectations which contradicted those they held in the past. These contradictions, through making incompatible demands on the Catawbas and the people with whom they had dealings, produced social conflict. Although social conflict is difficult to quantify, my impression is that social conflict increased among the Catawbas in direct proportion to their assimilation into the larger society. In trying to explain some of the changes that occurred after 1940, one of my informants told me that the changes were prompted by "restlessness."

The thing that has made the difference with us is mixing in with others and getting new ideas. Restlessness is the desire to see what other jobs and places are like. This began about 1938. This was working on the people who asked for the changes. They wanted to get under the Federal Government so they would have more chances. They were tired of the same old teacher in the same old school house.

My informant used "restlessness" to refer both to new values and expectations and to the social conflict they engendered. From 1940 until the early 1960's, the Catawbas were increasingly at odds with themselves and with outsiders.

Social conflict between Catawbas and outsiders commonly occurred in two social situations. The first situation in which conflict was frequent occurred when Catawbas tried to secure the rights of white citizens while retaining the considerable privileges of being Indian, the most important of which was being exempt from property taxes. The second situation occurred when external agencies attempted to help or assist the Catawbas in a way that demanded communal cooperation. In general, outsiders expected them to be more "Indian" than they were. Thus, the Catawbas came into conflict with outsiders when they tried to be too "white," and they also came into conflict when they were not "Indian" enough.

When the Catawbas first began working at the mills, we saw that white workers tried to keep them out on the grounds that they paid no property taxes. Similar conflict arose when the Catawbas began attending white schools, when they began riding on the school buses, and when they registered for voting. In all of these cases the Catawbas were assisted by Office of Indian Affairs officials who persuaded local officials to accept the Catawbas on the same basis as whites.

In the forties, a government man told some of the Indians to go up to the store and register to vote. But the people at the store wouldn't let them register, so they came back and told the government man. Then he went up to the store and made them allow them to register. But not many of the Indians vote today.

Some of my informants perceived an ulterior motive behind denial of rights because they paid no property taxes. When I asked one of my informants why the whites wanted to keep the Indians out of the public schools, he said: "The whites were just prejudiced; they wanted to hold the Indians back." However, regardless of what the real motives were, one source of conflict between Catawbas and whites arose through the Catawbas pressing for the rights of whites while retaining the privileges of Indians.

Another situation involving conflict occurred when outside groups and agencies tried to "do something" for the Catawbas. These outsiders typically had good motives, but their efforts to help usually failed. In general, the Catawba resented interference from the outside. One outsider who had long experience with the Catawbas said: "You have to work slowly with the Indians; the door is either open or closed, and if it is closed you are just out of luck." Outsiders typically expected the Catawbas to be naturally close and cooperative. An organization in Rock Hill, for example, once tried to set up a shop on the reservation to serve as an outlet for Catawba pottery. One of the potters summed it up this way:

They've tried several times to set up a shop for everybody, but it never worked out. No one wanted to be responsible for the pottery of other people. Some didn't finish theirs well, and it couldn't be sold for the same that the others sold it for. Some didn't burn it well enough. There are several problems. Some didn't want to sell at that shop. Some are careful and some are careless. Those that didn't burn it well enough—the pottery melts and this hurts the sale of the other potters.

At the time of my field work the pottery shop, a small rough building, stood deserted.

The Office of Indian Affairs inevitably encountered the same sort of conflict with the Catawbas. Because the Office of Indian Affairs held their land in trust, the Catawbas felt they did not have to cooperate if they did not wish to. "The Federal Government couldn't just come in and tell us what to do. We wouldn't toe the line for them." A few Catawbas, for example, continued to cut cord wood, Christmas trees, and pulp wood on the New Reservation even though it was illegal. Eventually, the Office of Indian Affairs withdrew its agent from the Reservation and administered the Catawbas from the Cherokee agency. One woman who worked for a social agency in Rock Hill said: "The people the Federal Government sent here just didn't understand the Catawbas."

In addition to conflict caused by contradictory expectations, there were other sources of conflict as the Catawbas progressively moved out into the white world. Some of it was clearly due to prejudice on the part of the whites. In one case, there was a white school bus driver who caused trouble.

He would stop for the white children, but he wouldn't stop for the Indians. Sometimes he would stop and sometimes he wouldn't. He would pull my little girl's pony tail when she got on the bus. I went and complained to an official. I started crying—and when I cry I am ready to fight. He wouldn't do anything about it. Then I went to another official and took several mothers with me. He looked into it, and in a little while we had a new bus driver.

In other cases the cause of conflict was not so much with white prejudice but with sensitivity on the part of the Catawbas. They often expected whites to be unsympathetic or hostile: "The Indians want to be left alone. They don't like whites to interfere. I have seen this towards me and towards others. They think the whites look down on them. They know that they are a different color, and they think the whites look down on them." This sensitivity is more characteristic of the older generation than of the younger generation. "Indians are not as friendly as white folks—this is mostly true of the older ones who went to all their schools here. The ones that are now going out to school will be easier to get along with."

Hand in hand with increasing conflict between Catawbas and outsiders, the Catawbas experienced increasing internal conflict which was further intensified by two contradictory value systems. On the one hand, the Catawbas traditionally valued communalism, emphasizing cooperation, generosity, and community solidarity. On the other hand, however, as the Catawbas were increasingly assimilated they began to value individualism, emphasizing advancement in their jobs, thrift, and conspicuous consumption.

In accordance with the old values, in the years following 1940 the Catawbas continued to think of themselves as an Indian community with strong solidarity. My informants frequently illustrated their belief in community solidarity by telling me about "workings," a form of voluntary labor. One man for example, told me about an incident where voluntary labor developed spontaneously: "When somebody builds something, everybody pitches in. I started building a home for my mother one morning, and by the end of the day 20 or 30 people were helping." Another informant gave me an example of community solidarity involving a man whose ancestors had left the reservation in the late nineteenth century. This man, a descendant of the Catawbas who emigrated to Colorado under the influence of Mormonism, returned to the reservation some years ago and was immediately accepted back into the tribe. My informant said that "anyone would have taken him in." Subsequently, the man's brother left Colorado and came to the reservation where he was accepted into the home of a "sixth or seventh cousin."

The Catawbas still retained their traditional belief in community cooperativeness and solidarity at the time I did field work. However, in the light of what I observed, their believed-in state of affairs was at variance with their real state of affairs; most of their cooperative endeavors failed. For example, I once attended a "social" which was organized for the purpose of raising funds for the church. As planned, the social was to feature entertainment by musicians, and money was to be raised by the sale of food and beverages. As it turned out, however, the musicians failed to appear, and the food and beverages sold slowly; even though prices were later reduced, most of it remained unsold when the social ended. On several occasions I overheard people discussing plans for picnics and workings, but these discussions often ended with no definite plans being made or with the decision to delay making plans until some future time. During my field work, the Catawbas succeeded in organizing only one working, and it was a rather unenthusiastic affair. One discussion of plans for a picnic ended with: "It seems like they don't want to get together any more." Several whites who worked for organizations that tried "to do something" for the Catawbas told me they were exceedingly difficult to organize: "the least spirit of cooperation you'll ever find."

Like any small, relatively closed community, the Catawbas were beset with a series of smouldering, petty feuds; the slightest incident could touch them off, igniting the community with open conflict. Lying beneath their traditional value system these feuds and animosities were both deep and long-standing. Conflict was particularly apt to break out between families.

Kinship was one of their biggest problems. That was why they began to intermarry with others [i.e., whites]. They were too close kin. It would go to aunts, uncles, and even to cousins. They were closer than people on the outside. If one was sick, even if it was a cousin, they would go and sit as if she was their own sister. They thought that their family could do no wrong. They were ready to fight if anybody said anything about their family. There's plenty of examples of even cousins [fighting

for each other]. This is not true for cousins now. They have
moved out a lot.[6]

Given these feuds and animosities in the context of a closed
community, almost anything could precipitate open conflict, even violence.

They used to try to settle their own disputes. Fist fights,
cutting scrapes. Drinking started it. Sometimes one family would
have a grudge against another. The church settled a lot of disputes. The elders would talk to the people. They would fall
out about things—like pitching horseshoes.

Conflicts also occurred within families, and these conflicts
ramified into other social situations. A Catawba who was
active in the church gave me an example: "When two sisters
quarrel, one of them will quit coming to church to take it out
on the other one." Another informant told me that she was
reluctant to assume responsibility for a Sunday school class
because if the children misbehaved she would have to report
them to the branch president of the church; their parents, of
course, were likely to be her kinsmen. Another woman told
me that she dreaded the beginning of school because the
children fought on the school buses, and this could cause
trouble between their parents.

It is probable that traditional Catawba society, being a
small, closed community, had no more internal conflict than
any other community with similar characteristics. However,
when the traditional, communalistic value system began to
be challenged by a new, individualistic value system, small
quarrels grew into large disputes. The new values were not
wholly unprecedented: "The Indians always wanted things;
they just didn't know how to get them." But they did not
adopt the new values overnight: "My husband used to say
that what was good enough for his parents is good enough
for us. It wasn't until our children were almost grown that
we realized that this wasn't true. When something becomes
a part of you, it is hard to get rid of it."

---

6. That is, the range of relatives included in the Catawba "family"
has shrunk; cousins are not thought to be as close as they previously
were.

The traditional value system persisted not through habit, however, but because it was fundamental in the organization of Catawba life. Social prestige, for example, was gained through being generous and helpful toward one's kinsmen and neighbors. A leader or a successful man did not set himself apart from his followers through conspicuous consumption; everybody was supposed to be more or less alike (Cf. Erasmus 1961:101-134). The last chief, for example, is remembered as having been a paragon of generosity. Before 1940 when a Catawba died the chief would always volunteer to haul the corpse into Rock Hill to an undertaker; he never charged a fee for this, "he always tried to help."

The old value system, encouraging everybody to be on a par with everybody else, was sanctioned by means of invidious gossip. When somebody became too ambitious, the others would say that he was "big-headed" or that he "thought he was better than everybody else." With economic development and the individualistic value system, invidious gossip increased: "In the old days there was nothing to be jealous about. They barely had enough to eat. It is different now. A lot of them will fuss about one having a big car or a new house or getting something on credit."

Several of my informants told me that where a white will compete with his neighbor in conspicuous consumption, an Indian will "talk his neighbor down," i.e., resort to invidious gossip.

Where whites will try to keep up with each other, the Indians will talk. They will say, "She acts like she is too good to talk to me." The Indians would be better off if they would try to keep up with one another instead of talking somebody down. I've heard a lot of them say that an Indian doesn't like to see another Indian get ahead.

Thus, as economic development and assimilation proceeded, the Catawbas came to hold two contradictory value systems. When a Catawba, impelled by the individualistic value system, began to show signs of material success, his kinsmen and neighbors "talked him down" in terms of the traditional, communalistic value system. In some instances, the Catawbas accused successful people of getting ahead at their expense, the implication being that the successful ones had somehow advanced themselves by cheating the unsuccessful ones.

In this conflict-ridden situation the Office of Indian Affairs attempted to institute a tribal council structured as an impersonal bureaucracy, with formally elected officials having specific rights and duties. In the traditional political system the council had been composed of elected officials, but their terms in office had been somewhat indefinite; once elected, a man stayed in office until he was "put out." In the traditional system, the elections had been informal, usually having the appearance of being unanimous.

They didn't much want to be elected. They wouldn't push hard. They used a hand vote. It didn't matter how many people were there. There was seldom any opposition. One man wanted to be chief, but he got in trouble and his people wouldn't support him.

Apparently the council also resolved issues by informal means. When they could not decide an issue, they took it to an outside magistrate for settlement. The magistrate then advised the Indians about the matter, usually encouraging them to return to the reservation and try to settle it among themselves. If this failed they again took it to the magistrate who then handed down a decision.

In place of this informal system, the Office of Indian Affairs instituted a council governed by a formal constitution and by-laws. The preamble to the constitution reads:

We, the members of the Catawba Indian Tribe of South Carolina, in order to set up a more effective tribal organization, to improve our social and economic welfare, and to secure to ourselves and our posterity the benefits of organization, do hereby establish and ordain this constitution and by-laws for the Catawba IndianTribe.[7]

Under the constitution, the Catawba tribal council consisted of five officers: a chief, an assistant chief, a secretary-treasurer, and two trustees. The first council took office in July 1944; subsequently, elections were held in the July general meeting of every even-numbered year.

---

7. *Constitution and By-Laws of the Catawba Indian Tribe of South Carolina*, approved June 30, 1944 (Washington, D. C.: U. S. Government Printing Office, 1946), p. 1.

The council was empowered to negotiate with the local, state, and federal governments. It was responsible for passing and enforcing ordinances pertaining to the supervision and management of reservation lands, and it was responsible for protecting the wildlife and natural resources on the reservation. The council, for example, passed a regulation making it illegal to cut timber on the New Reservation except for use as fuel and building materials; the cutting of timber for sale as cord wood, pulp wood, and Christmas trees was specifically prohibited.

The old tribal council had settled issues informally; in the new council, elected officers were required to enforce regulations in formal meetings whose proceedings were recorded by the secretary-treasurer. Through being required to take definite stands on issues and decisions, the members of the council were often caught in double binds. According to the traditional value system they were supposed to support their relatives, but according to the constitution and by-laws they were supposed to reach decisions impartially, even when their relatives were involved. Thus, the officials were frequently accused of being partial to their relatives.

Jealousy and greediness, to speak plainly. You would put in a group of executives and they would aid their people instead of being fair to all. You will start thinking that a person is not treating you fair, and soon you believe that it is real. At one time, there were three on the council from one family: an uncle and two nephews. That was it right there. They would create jobs to suit their own family needs.

In addition to charges of being partial to relatives, the officials were often charged with acting out of self-interest. One informant explained how the charge of self-interest disrupted things:

They had problems before they divided up the land. When it came to doing something for the tribe they would just think of themselves. They couldn't get together. If someone suggested something, they would say that it was just for him and not for the tribe. They were afraid that another Indian might get ahead.

The councilmen never worked for the tribe. They were always for themselves. When the new land was bought, some of them got tracts of land with houses on them. Others just got tracts of land. The councilmen got houses and the others didn't. That put them ahead right there.

The Catawbas could not easily conceive of impersonal, disinterested decisions; in their way of thinking, decisions were likely to be prompted either by self-interest or partiality towards kinsmen.

The two issues that divided the Catawbas most deeply were the cutting of timber on reservation lands and the communal cattle project. As we have seen, one of the traditional occupations of Catawbas had been cutting and selling cord wood and Christmas trees. Under the new regulations, however, this became illegal. Nonetheless, several Catawbas continued to cut timber on reservation lands. Those who cut the timber felt that the regulation was unreasonable, their argument being that the people who cut the timber were needy.

They [the tribal council] seemed like they owned the reservation and everybody on it. They seemed to tell everybody what to do. A lot would tell you what you could and couldn't do. Some Indians just won't let another Indian tell them what to do. These people never did like for anybody to tell them what to do.

Like when that council member stopped them from selling trees. They were saying that they belonged to the Federal Government, but they didn't. They were held in trust for the Indians. One man that cut them was sick, on welfare. Several of them cut a few cedars to get toys for their children. The council member met the man in town and told him that the trees were off of Federal property; it scared him to death.

On at least one occasion, members of the tribal council called in law officers to prevent some of the Catawbas from selling Christmas trees that had already been cut. This reliance on external officials to sanction a purely internal problem was an admission, as it were, that they had internal conflicts that they could not resolve by existing means.

The communal cattle project was another source of conflict that "strained" the structure of Catawba society. When it became apparent that the Catawbas were not going to take up individual farming, the Office of Indian Affairs sponsored a communally operated cattle project. The tribal council was empowered to appoint one or two men to take care of the cattle. After the cattle were sold the profits were to be equally divided among all the Catawbas. Although the project eventually became economically sound, it stimulated a series of disputes. The Catawbas disagreed over who could decide to sell the cattle and when they were to be sold. Almost inevitably, members of the tribal council were accused of self-interest in filling the jobs of tending the cattle.

It benefited four or five families and none of the others. The chief benefited off of the cattle. We voted to sell them and he didn't do it. I asked him why, and he said the prices were low. He went out to take care of them. Another man used to take care of them because he was down in health. The chief just pretended he was looking after them; he didn't, but he still got paid. He was working at the mill at that time. I think that different families should have taken turns in taking care of them.

These two issues above all the others demonstrated to the Catawbas that there were serious contradictions and conflicts in their social structure. In the words of an old Catawba man: "Everybody got divided up."

Economic and cultural development introduced a series of organizational changes in the Catawba way of life, and it introduced an individualistic value system. Although these changes generally improved their standard of living, the Catawbas paid an initial price. As we have seen, the changes both intensified existing conflicts and introduced new sources of conflict. Disputes and misunderstandings mounted in intensity until they exceeded the structural resources of Catawba society. Issues arose that could only be resolved by firm decisions on the part of the tribal council. Yet, regardless of what decision the council reached, the council members were criticized as being partial or self-interested, and it was not at all uncommon for a council member to be accused of both. Eventually, the tribal council was disrupted by a series of resignations. For example, two out of the last three Catawba chiefs resigned after serving short terms in office. Resignation was their only means of escaping the double binds that were intrinsic to their offices.

To make matters worse, neither the State of South Carolina nor the Office of Indian Affairs was clear about its responsibilities toward the Catawbas. For example, by the late 1950's many of the Catawbas had acquired automobiles; however, the usefulness of these vehicles was hampered because the dirt roads on the reservation became impassable in wet weather. When the Catawbas tried to have paved roads put on the reservation, they found that neither South Carolina nor the Office of Indian Affairs was sure whose responsibility it was to pave the roads.

This conflict was caused by contradictions in Catawba social structure: the only way they could reduce it was to change the structure of their society, and this is what they did. On January 3, 1959, the Catawbas passed a resolution requesting that a bill be introduced to Congress allowing them to divide their assets and terminate their status as Indians. Their way of reducing conflict was to divest themselves of that which required them to cooperate. However, because some of the Catawbas said that they had not been informed of the meeting in which this resolution was passed, they decided to hold a second meeting and take another vote.

The Catawbas who were opposed to termination argued that although termination was inevitable, the people were not prepared for it. They predicted that if the Catawbas got title to their land, it would all be sold within six months. Some of the Catawbas argued that they could not afford to give up the advantages of free medical services and tax-free lands. Still others said that if the lands were sold, anybody could move in and "build houses on top of each other," a practice which would irritate Catawbas who were accustomed to living in rather widely spaced houses.

The arguments of those who were in favor of termination were somewhat more positive. The most prevalent argument in favor of termination was that if they had deeds to their lands, they could borrow money to improve their homes. Others said that they were "fed up" with being wards of the government; they wanted to pay taxes like everybody else so they "could hold up their heads and look the world in the face."

In March 1959 the Catawbas held a second meeting which was attended by representatives from the state, officials from the Office of Indian Affairs, representatives from other interested organizations, and 60 eligible Catawba voters. When a second vote was taken to introduce a termination bill to Congress, it passed by a margin of 40 in favor to 17 opposed, 3 voters abstaining.

Before a final tribal roll could be compiled, the status of Catawba-white marriages had to be clarified. Under the South Carolina miscegenation law of 1879, marriages between Indians and whites were illegal and the children of such unions were not legitimate. However, in spite of this law we have seen that Catawba-white intermarriage increased sharply after 1940. One of the officials of the Office of Indian Affairs had raised this marriage issue in 1958 when he reported that 120 out of 162 Catawba families contained one white spouse.[8] South Carolina lawmakers introduced to the House of Representatives and the Senate a bill making the marriages legal; the bill became a law in April, 1960.[9]

The final tribal roll was closed out on July 2, 1960. This roll includes all surviving Catawbas who were on the July 1, 1943, roll drawn up when the New Reservation was purchased. It also includes the Catawbas who were residents of South Carolina but were absent while serving in the armed forces on July 1, 1943. Finally, it includes the children of these two categories of people who were residents of South Carolina when their children were born. The final roll includes 631 persons in all.

The actual division of the reservation was governed by the following rules. Every Catawba on the roll had the right to choose his portion of the settlement either in land or money. The head of a family could decide whether his minor children would receive land or money. (1) First choice to particular tracts of land went to Catawbas who had land assignments. That is, they could choose to take the land on which they were living, provided, of course, that it did not exceed their share. (2) Catawbas who decided to take their settlement in land could choose any unassigned land.

---

8. *Charlotte Observer*, Charlotte, North Carolina, January 5, 1960.

9. Code of Laws of South Carolina, 1962, Title 20, Chapter 1, Article 1, Sections 20-27, pp. 120-121. The new law applied specifically to Catawbas, while still prohibiting marriage between a white on the one hand, and a "mulatto, half-breed, Indian, Negro or mestizo" on the other.

When several members of a single family chose land, they attempted to select contiguous tracts. (3) The Catawbas who chose a money settlement were to receive a share of cash from the sale of land that was not claimed by other Catawbas. (4) Finally, the Catawbas who wanted to purchase tracts of land could do so by meeting the highest bid on the tract of land in which they were interested.

According to Bureau of Indian Affairs figures, there were 3,434.3 acres to be divided. From this, a 35 acre tract of land on which the school, church, and playground were located and a 100 acre tract that included a fish pond were set aside. These 135 acres were given in trust to the Catawba Mormon church. Out of 631 on the roll, 262 selected a money settlement, and the remainder chose land. In June 1962 the 1,433 acres of unclaimed land was sold and the proceeds equally divided among the Catawbas who chose money. Termination proceedings were final on July 1, 1962.

When I asked the Catawbas about the effects of termination, I encountered a variety of appraisals. Some of them felt that termination was clearly beneficial; for the first time, many of the Catawbas owned their homes and had the means to make repairs and improvements. One man said that since termination was inevitable, they were wise in having done it when they did: "If we had waited much longer before dividing up, there wouldn't have been much to go around." Some took a more moderate view, saying that termination had benefited the young, but that it had adversely affected some of the old people.

Some of the Catawbas felt that termination was a mistake. In particular, they felt that having to pay for medical services was going to be a hardship for many people. "This is the first time in a hundred years that there is no doctor. It is going to be a hardship. Doesn't seem so right now, but it will be. Good many got land, and some got money. But they'll find out after a while that they have no money and no doctor."

Some of those who felt that termination was a mistake emphasized that many of the Catawbas who chose land have since sold it. "A lot of them sold their land before they had the deeds. I was in town putting our children's money in the bank, and they were walking up and down the streets spend-

ing theirs. They didn't speak to us until after they had spent
their money."

It is perhaps significant, however, that some of those who
felt that termination was a mistake did not feel that there
was a need for reinstating a tribal council. Most of the
Catawbas, whether they were for or against termination, did
not feel that the tribal council should be reinstated.

In explaining why termination occurred, many Catawbas
emphasized the role of outsiders. They said that several whites
had come in and expressed their opposition to termination
because "they were afraid we would get out and get something." Some said that they terminated because they "got too
close to the whites." By a variety of means many of the
Catawbas attempted to deflect responsibility for termination
on outsiders. This is, of course, particularly true of the
Catawbas who felt that termination was a mistake.

At the time of my field work the two things that still
served to hold the Catawbas together—albeit tenuously—were
the Old Reservation and the Mormon church. The 630 acre
Old Reservation was still held in trust by South Carolina.
Several Catawba families continued to live on the Old Reservation just as they did before termination. For others, it was a
source of security. In an emergency, such as prolonged illness,
they could move back to the Old Reservation where they
would at least have a place to live. Some families who managed
their settlement poorly had already moved back.

A more important social bond was the church. There
were, however, some indications that the church was less
influential than it was in the past. "I can remember when
everybody went to church; now they say they can take it
or leave it." One factor in the decline of church membership
was the establishment of a second Mormon church in Rock
Hill in 1962. The membership of the two churches was divided by U. S. Highway 21. All of those to the west of the
highway went to the church in Rock Hill, while all those
to the east went to the Catawba church. Both Indians and
whites went to the church in Rock Hill, but because the
reservation lies to the east of Highway 21, the Catawba
membership was largely Indian.

For the church on the reservation the most important
loss caused by this division in the congregation was not the

numerical loss of members; it was the loss of outsiders. A member of the Catawba church explained it this way:

There used to be quite a few white members here who came in from town. They were the leaders; they were very active. After they divided the church, they had to attend in town. After the whites left, our Relief Society dropped off a lot. There were two or three whites and two or three Indians, and they worked together. Now, all they have are Indians. They can't work together. There's always some beef. I can work with any of them, but a lot of them can't. A lot of them won't attend if there is one leader they don't like.

Here is but another expression of the fundamental contradictions in Catawba society. The same forces that led to termination were producing dissension and poor attendance in church.

CHAPTER VI

The Residue of Time

THE first part of this study is now complete. In preceding chapters we have examined the social process which began with the Catawbas as an obscure aboriginal society, saw them subsequently incorporated into the plural structure of South Carolina society, and ended with their terminating their status as Indians with the Bureau of Indian Affairs. We have viewed a series of human actions and events with attempted objectivity. Turning now to the second part of this study, we shall examine the folk history of the Catawbas, the residue of human actions and events in the minds of living people.

Being concerned with the memory of the past rather than the past itself, the account in the following pages is in several respects different from "universal history," history in the usual sense. While universal history takes the form of narrative, or at least a series of events anchored in chronology, folk history takes the form of a series of themes analytically derived from empirical data. These themes are general propositions about the past which are logically prior to the beliefs, perceptions, and actions of a particular group of people (Cf. Cunnison 1951).

Moreover, it has not been appropriate to verify the historical beliefs presented in this chapter in the way universal historical statements are verified. The role they play in the social context in which they occur is more relevant than the accuracy with which they represent the past. We shall presently see that the historical process set forth in preceding chapters has left residues in the minds of Indians and whites that do not precisely mesh. That is to say, the Indians and the whites agree on the broad outlines of Catawba history, but they do not agree on details, and for the student of society the differences are as relevant as the similarities. From an omniscient point of view, Catawba history is a single unique process; but to the descendants of the people who participated in this history, it has been refracted by social structure, as it were, into two differently colored versions.

CATAWBA HISTORY: WHITE VERSION

The version of Catawba history that has become incapsulated[1] in the minds of whites is structured around three general themes: (1) the Catawbas are descended from Indians; (2) the Catawbas were friends of the colonists; and (3) the Catawbas are the remnant of a once great nation. Although these themes do not exhaustively account for all details of the white version of Catawba history, they are logically consistent with much of what the whites say about the Catawbas, with many of their actual dealings with the Catawbas, and to some extent with their perception of the Catawbas.

The most fundamental theme in the white version of Catawba history is the belief that the ancestors of the Catawbas were Indians. I do not use "Indian" here in a technical sense. Indeed, it is doubtful that the term can have a technical sense except in a very general way. The aboriginal inhabitants of the New World were diverse in every respect —racially, linguistically, culturally, and socially. They were so diverse that "Indian" can have no precise meaning. Nonetheless, in the minds of Americans the word designates a meaningful historical distillate—a stereotype (Hallowell 1957).

The white neighbors of the Catawbas believe that the ancient Catawbas lived in much the way that most Americans believe Indians lived. They believe, for example, that the ancient Catawbas were members of a discrete, nominate social group. They were a self-contained, independent nation. One white informant, for example, told me in all sincerity that this was true until very recently.

No enforcement officer could set foot on that reservation to arrest any one. They just began to do it several years ago. If a man committed a crime, all he had to do was reach that place.

---

1. E. E. Evans-Pritchard (1962) was the first anthropologist to use this apt term, and I have retained his spelling for consistency.

It was an Indian Nation—no enforcement officer could go there. We used to be woke up at two or three o'clock in the morning by some criminal looking for the reservation. They have only had an agreement with enforcement officers for about fifteen or twenty years.

This is, of course, an exaggerated expression of the belief that modern Catawbas retain something of the independent national status that their ancestors enjoyed in full measure, but many whites hold this belief to a lesser extent.

The whites believe that the ancient Catawbas, like other Indians, vested authority in males, and that they were led by a powerful chief, a venerable old man. This belief colored their perception of Chief Blue, the last of the traditional Catawba chiefs. In turn Chief Blue was undoubtedly aware of these beliefs, using them as points of reference in shaping his "Indian" role for the benefit of outsiders. A white informant gave me the following description of the image Blue projected.

You should have known Chief Blue. By being put out on their own, a lot of them don't know what has happened. Chief Blue was liked by everybody. He would come in on a horse, visiting around. He liked to talk. He was a very dynamic person. He could lead them—that is what they lack now. When Blue sold cord wood, he made friends he never forgot.

Chief Blue was the one. You would see him come into town with leather trousers and a headdress. His wife would follow him like a puppy dog. If you asked her a question, she would say, "ask my husband."

Because Chief Blue was the last speaker of the Catawba language and because he reputedly had a large number of children, the whites thought of him as the "last of the ancient Catawbas." For this reason, they thought that the other Catawbas respected him to a man, following his advice and decisions without reservation. This, of course, was not true, particularly after the tribal council was reorganized in 1943.

In many ways, white people thought of Chief Blue as a living symbol of their version of Catawba history. While the Catawbas were in the process of termination, whites in Rock Hill produced a historical drama, *Kah-Woh, Catawba*, dealing with the relation between the Catawbas and the colonists

(Long 1960). Chief Blue, playing himself, appears in the opening and closing scenes of the drama as a venerable old man entertaining a group of children with stories about the ancient Catawbas. When a quarrel develops among the children over which of them are his grandchildren, he explains in accordance with the white stereotype that he is probably grandfather to all of them because he fathered no less than twenty-three children. According to the genealogy I collected, Chief Blue fathered ten children, only seven of whom produced grandchildren.

The whites believed that the ancient Catawbas possessed superior physiques but child-like intelligence. More precisely, they are thought to have been physically superior not in their capacity to do hard work, but in such pursuits as hunting and athletics. The whites firmly believe that the ancient Catawbas were hunters rather than agriculturists.

The most mistaken idea is that the reservation land is poor. It is not. They kept the trees down for fuel. When we set the Negroes free, they knew how to farm, but the Indians could only hunt and fish. They never stayed in one place long enough to build homes. The only thing they could do was make pottery, and they can't make very good pottery.

This belief explains why the Catawbas did not farm the New Reservation lands. When I told one white man that James Adair had seen a large Catawba corn field in the eighteenth century, he could not believe it.

The Negroes lived along with white men and learned their agricultural techniques, while the Indians were shut off. In this way, the Negroes got ahead. The Federal Government expected the Indians to become farmers, but they did not know how to farm. They were working in the mills. Individual farming didn't work. Then they tried collective farming, and that didn't work either.

As further confirmation of this belief, whites told me about two or three Catawba boys who have been outstanding football players. The athletic ability of these boys is beyond doubt; all were offered substantial athletic scholarships by universities. However, I feel that their being Indians gave them an aura of ferociousness that a white athlete of equal ability would not have had.

An example of belief in the limited intellectual capabilities of Indians was given me by a white man who once led a Boy Scout troop including both whites and Catawbas. He explained to me that the Indians made excellent campers, but they were limited in their ability to master the Boy Scout Manual. None ever got past the second grade of scouting. The belief that the Indians were not adept in intellectual matters explains why they cannot manage their money well. "They give money to their children for candy when they should spend it on clothing. They drive cars while living in shacks and carrying their water."

The belief that ancient Indians are ancestral to modern Indians, the former shaping the stereotype of the latter, is probably held in some degree by most Americans, but the white neighbors of the Catawbas have an additional belief that is probably a Southern phenomenon. That is, they believe there has historically been a natural antipathy between Catawbas and Negroes. Undoubtedly, this belief is a residue of the social position of the Catawbas in plural South Carolina. On numerous occasions whites told me that there has always been a natural enmity between the Catawbas and Negroes. The Catawbas are believed to have always had a natural distaste for Negroes, always keeping socially distinct from them. The Negroes, on the other hand, are believed to have always been naturally afraid of the Catawbas.

This belief frequently comes into play when the "racial purity" of the Catawbas is for some reason questioned. It was, for example, part of South Carolina's justification for giving aid to the Catawbas. The following passage is from the report to the South Carolina Senate describing the acquisition of the New Reservation.

Not now, nor at any time in the past, has there been social intermingling between the Catawbas and negroes [sic]. An aged Indian says that so far as he knows, not a drop of negro blood has ever flowed in the veins of a Catawba Indian. When asked how the Catawbas and negroes got along, this Indian replied: "Fine. We have nothing to do with them, and they have nothing to do with us. There hasn't been a negro on the Reservation in five years." Very few full-blooded Indians are left among the Catawbas. Most of them are half-breeds (Bradford n.d.: 15).

White admixture was deplored, perhaps, but admixture with Negroes would almost certainly have disqualified the Catawbas from receiving state aid. The social position of the Catawbas depended upon both their being descended from Indians and not being mixed with Negroes.

The white neighbors of the Catawbas, like most Americans, believe that there were two kinds of Indians in the Colonial era: friendly and hostile. The whites believe that of all the Southeastern Indians the Catawbas were the best friends the colonists had. The Catawbas violated this friendship only once, when during the Yamassee War they attacked the colonists. In the play *Kah-Woh, Catawba*, however, even this was atoned for when one of the white characters in the play explains to President Washington how the whites gained possession of the territory of the Waxhaw Indians.

This area at one time belonged to the Waxhaw Indians. It's a very interesting story. The only time the Catawbas ever sided against the whites was during the Yamassee War, and then for only a short while. It seems that they were so ashamed of this one action against the whites that they withdrew and went to Charleston to ask forgiveness. The Governor told them they would be pardoned if they would do something about quieting the Waxhaw Indians and try to make them stop molesting the whites. Well, the Catawbas came here and wiped out the Waxhaws almost to a man (Long 1960:60).

Afterwards, so the story goes, the whites began to settle Waxhaw territory, all the dirty work having been done by shame-ridden Catawbas.

To a detached observer this belief in the friendship between whites and Catawbas is curiously unrealistic in its not being reciprocal. The whites always got more out of the relationship than the Catawbas. It is this aspect of the friendship, for example, that explains how the first white man came to settle on Catawba land.

The Catawba Indians found him . . . and "they got around him and strongly persuaded, and almost forced him to set his stakes there." They told him they would give him all the land he wanted . . . and finally prevailed upon him to remain on the spot where he had camped that night (Brown 1953:60).

This concept of friendship also accounts for the aid the

Catawbas gave the whites in the American Revolution and in the Civil War. The implication of the belief is that the Catawbas, perhaps regarding the whites as their "brothers," spontaneously and naturally assisted them, demanding little or nothing in return.

Believing as they do in the selfless friendship of the Catawbas, it is at first curious that the whites do not feel guilty or even responsible for having taken away their land. Actually, the whites have two ways of deflecting responsibility away from themselves. One way of doing this is to argue an evolutionary theory.

The wild land belonged to him who was most willing to cultivate it for its greatest usefulness. The hunter must give way to the herdsman, and the herdsman to the cultivator of the soil. This had proved to be the law of progress, and the laws of civilized nations accepted its immutability. It is a law of nature (Brown 1953:54).

Thus, even though the Catawbas trusted the whites, extending to them their friendship, the whites were inevitably to take their land. Being governed by a law of nature, the dispossession of the Catawbas was untempered by morality; it was nobody's fault that they lost their land.

Another way of deflecting responsibility is to argue that the Indians lost their land because they were incapable of managing it, having the mentality of children, and because there were a *few* unscrupulous whites who took advantage of their ineptness. That is what is supposed to have happened after the Catawbas began leasing their lands.

But in the course of time they were allowed to take the collection of rents into their own hands; then all went into chaos and confusion. Many, like Sam Scott, for instance, would take a bottle of whiskey for their whole year's rent, and many white men would do business with them in that way until it became an intolerable disgrace to the country (Brown 1953:62).

Thus, the whites admit that some whites—"white trash"— were guilty of cheating the Catawbas, but they themselves, not being descended from "white trash," are immune from guilt.

In recent years, the whites have invoked the friendship theme as a justification for giving aid to the Catawbas.

Various associations in Rock Hill, for example, occasionally thought it would be a good thing to repay past favors by "doing something for the Indians." In addition, we have seen that the ostensible motive of South Carolina in buying the New Reservation was to repay the Catawbas for favors they did for the whites in the past (Bradford n.d.: 13).

The basic theme of *Kah-Woh, Catawba* is the friendship between the Catawbas and the colonists. As the play closes, President Washington is confronted by one of the Catawba headmen who recounts the help that the Catawbas had given to the colonists. The Catawba then complains about illicit white encroachments onto their reservation. Washington, suddenly taking the role of bureaucrat, says: "This is a matter to take up with the Superintendent of Indian Affairs for this area." He then gives the Catawba a medal, saying: "Kah-woh, Speaking not only for myself but for all the people of these United States, I should like to say, 'Kah-woh, Catawba'." Washington's final utterance is supposed to mean, "thank you, people of the river" (Long 1960:92-93).

The whites believe that modern Catawbas are a remnant, having declined from an aboriginal condition of greatness and power. Thus, the whites believe that Catawba history from the colonial era to the present has been shaped by decline or decadence. This belief explains why modern Catawbas are so different from stereotyped Indians. It also explains why few of the Catawbas have "pride." According to white informants, Chief Blue was about the only Catawba who was "proud."

Chief Blue had the good will of a lot of people. He would go to the legislature every year. He was always willing to dress up in his furry headgear and show you how they used to look. The others wouldn't do it. Last Christmas we made costumes for the Indian children for a float. It would have stolen the show. But one of the Indians said that they should be in school or on the playground. The least spirit of cooperation you'll ever find. I don't know what will become of them.

Saying that the Indians have no "pride" means, I think, that they do not want to behave the way whites expect them to behave. Chief Blue was different; as we have seen, he played an "Indian" role to further the interests of the Catawbas and his own interests as well. A white woman said to me: "He did a lot to keep the Indians together; he took a lot of pride in being Indian. A lot do not—they want to get out and act like anybody else [i.e., like whites]."

Decline or decadence is a major theme in *Kah-woh, Catawba*. In the conversation between the Catawba headman and President Washington, the headman says:

I have tried to encourage our people and to rebuild something of the past, but my people are beaten down and depressed. Our once great nation of many thousand warriors has dwindled to a mere handful, due to many epidemics of smallpox, fighting other Indians to help protect ourselves and our white brothers, drinking the poisonous liquors sold to our people by the white man. We have lost everything in our attempt to live in a White man's world, according to his ways (Long 1960:92).

Some of the whites interpret termination as perhaps the final step in the long decline of the Catawbas. One white person told me that if Chief Blue had been alive, the Catawbas would not have terminated. Actually, Chief Blue was in favor of termination.

To summarize, these three themes are general propositions about Catawba history incapsulated in the minds of whites. They do not, of course, account for all of the beliefs that whites have about Catawbas, nor are they held to an equal degree by all whites. Some whites told me that the Indians, far from declining, have improved greatly in the past 15 years. One man confided that he did not think that Chief Blue was quite as "Indian" as most people thought he was. Another told me that the Catawbas were not as naively friendly and helpful as they are made out to be, explaining that they sided with the Confederacy in the Civil War only after a white man told them that if they did not enlist they would be killed.

CATAWBA HISTORY: CATAWBA VERSION

We have just seen that the whites have "selected" certain aspects from the stream of Catawba history and incapsulated them into their belief system. We shall now see that the Catawbas have likewise "selected" aspects of this history, incapsulating them into quite a different belief system. The dominant themes in the Catawba view of their own history are: (1) the belief that they are descended from "Lamanites"; (2) the belief that they were too friendly toward the white colonists; (3) the belief that the Mormon missionaries were the first Christians who helped them; and (4) the belief that they have progressed.

Like the whites, the Catawbas believe that their ancestors were members of a discrete, nominate Indian society, and they likewise deny the possibility of Negro admixture, however slight. There is no way of determining whether these beliefs developed independently among whites and Catawbas, or whether one borrowed them from the other. However, some closely associated beliefs which the Catawbas hold are clearly borrowed from whites. In some cases the Catawbas have gotten these beliefs directly or indirectly from anthropologists. Some Catawbas say, for example, that they are descended from the "Sioux tribe." "The story is that the Catawbas were abandoned by the Sioux tribe because they were so savage. The Catawbas used to fight all the time. That's why they were never friendly with the Cherokees. Only one or two (Cherokees) have married in."

This belief in being descended from the "Sioux tribe" undoubtedly comes from Mooney's work (1894). The Catawbas could have learned this from anthropologists who have worked with them or from reading feature stories in newspapers. I know of only one instance where this belief affected a decision. In 1956 the relatives of a man named George R. Grey who claimed to be a "Sioux Indian" got in touch with the Catawbas. In accordance with Grey's wishes to be buried with the Sioux, his relatives asked the Catawbas if they would accept his body in their cemetery. The Catawbas, believing in their being descended from the "Sioux tribe," complied; subsequently, Grey's body was shipped from his home in New York State to the Old Reservation. It now lies in a corner of the old cemetery, somewhat removed from Catawba graves.

The Catawbas also tell a story about their ancestors having moved from Canada to their present location. Apparently, this story first appeared in the work of Henry Schoolcraft (Mooney 1894:69). I recorded one particularly elaborate version of this story:

According to tradition, the Catawbas came from Canada. Like other people, they were looking for a better place to live. They found the Carolinas from the mountains to the ocean full of game to feed themselves and their families. Their main trade was in pottery. They made this pottery and traded it to other Indians for blankets, bows and arrows, baskets, and anything else that was useful. It was made so well that it could be used to cook in. It would hold water.

There was a Catawba brave who took some pottery [to another tribe] to trade for bows and arrows. This chief [of the other tribe] had a beautiful daughter, and the Catawba brave fell in love with her, and she likewise fell in love with him. When the Catawba brave left, she asked her father for a bow and arrow. She shot it in the air in the direction the brave went, and then she went to get it. She kept shooting it in the air until she caught up with him.

This caused trouble and a war between the two tribes. The other tribe must have been Cherokees. The chief claimed that the Catawbas had stolen his daughter and the bow and arrow. Naturally, this caused a lot of bloodshed and sorrow for both tribes.

The Catawba chief had the first peace pipe made from pottery with four stems.[2] The two chiefs that were at war and two other chiefs smoked the pipe. There are Indian heads on both sides of the pipe. These represent the two chiefs.

The boy and girl went off to themselves. They raised a lot of children which were very small and dark and wild. They lived in holes in trees. At night they would come out and scare the other Indian women and children. Then there was a flood in 1916, and this killed all the wild Indians.

Although several Catawbas told me origin stories, my impression is that they are not greatly interested in their origin. For example, the informant who told the above story carefully emphasized its being a "fairy tale," something not to be taken seriously.

With respect to their origin, the one thing on which virtually all Catawbas agree is that their ultimate ancestors were "Lamanites," a group of apostate Hebrews who came

---

2. These "peace pipes" are still made by Catawba potters. They are made in the form of a large bowl supported by three short legs; around the bowl, there are four stems arranged like the cardinal points of a compass.

to the New World, subsequently becoming the Indians of American history. This belief is, of course, one of the tenets of Mormon theology (O'Dea 1957:22). Even though most of the Catawbas share this belief, they do not elaborate upon it. One Catawba informant who was particularly bored with the question of origin, said: "I've heard that they belonged to another tribe. The Six Nations, I think. I guess the old ones knew where they came from."

For the social anthropologist the most significant thing about Catawba origin beliefs is their relative lack of interest in them. In contrast, some of the mestizos mentioned in earlier chapters of this study have a marked interest in their own origins. This is particularly true of the mestizos who are trying to gain recognition as Indians. For example, the mestizos of Robeson County, North Carolina, have changed their account of their origin at least four times in the past fifty years; with each change, they have adopted a different name (Berry 1963:152-161).

As we have seen, an important theme in the white version of Catawba history is the unselfish, even naive friendship of the Catawbas for the white colonists. The Catawbas agree that their ancestors were friends of the white colonists, but they say in contrast that their ancestors made the mistake of being too friendly. A Catawba man explained to me why the Federal Government did not give the Catawbas the aid they promised when the New Reservation was acquired:

Because the Catawbas fought with [i.e., were allied with] the United States, they never signed a treaty. The other ones, like the Cherokees, fought against the United States; they signed a treaty and now they get better schools. Some say that the Catawbas would be better off if they had fought against the United States.

Like the whites the Catawbas believe that their ancestors were friendly toward the white colonists, but unlike the whites they emphasize the one-sidedness of the relationship.

The Catawbas invoked this historical belief when they visited the South Carolina Legislature to solicit more aid. They began by recounting their unreciprocated friendship toward the colonists and their having been cheated out of their land by whites; they ended by saying it was high time the whites reciprocated their friendship and atoned for the wrongs done by unscrupulous "white trash." Moreover, this belief in unreciprocated friendship is a rationale for the Catawba's feeling of separateness, and in some cases their hostility toward the Federal Government. I heard several stories about Catawbas who got into trouble after publicly expressing their resentment toward the Federal Government.

The beliefs we have just examined refer to events and conditions in the remote past. The coming of the Mormon elders is a more recent event that has left an important residue in the belief system of modern Catawbas. In their folk history, it is perhaps the most crucial single event in their past.

My grandparents on both sides were among the first members of the church. My mother had a picture of the first elders to come here, but it is gone now. I don't remember the names of the first elders to come here. They would come here and stay with the people. They would also go out and work with neighboring whites. But they came among the Indians first; there were no Mormon churches in South Carolina at that time. They were the first Christians to come in and try to do anything for the Indians.

The Catawbas believe that the Mormons were the first Christians who were genuinely interested in their welfare. According to tradition before the elders came, a few Catawbas attended a Methodist Church near the reservation: "But they weren't treated well. They had to sit on back seats or stand outside."

In their account of the coming of the elders, the Catawbas are quite aware that they defied local whites in accepting Mormonism, but their motive for accepting it was not defiance. They accepted Mormonism because the Mormons were the first to take an interest in their spiritual and moral condition.

When the outsiders found that the missionaries were here, they fought them. They didn't bother the Indians, just the missionaries. My father and mother said they mobbed the first elders who came in here. They caught them and whipped both of them. They tried to make them drink some whiskey. They brought the elders to the line and sent them back to the reservation after they whipped them and made them promise to leave the next day. They tried to get them to promise not to come back, but they would not promise. They did leave the next day, according to promise.

I don't know how long they were gone, but they came back disguised, and the Indians had to meet them. Two Indians met them above Rock Hill near a Presbyterian church. They brought them back to the reservation. I don't know how long they stayed. As soon as outsiders found they were here, they sent a mob in here to run them out. The mob went to where the elders were staying, and the elders ran into the woods to prevent another whipping. They shot at them when they ran. One man was sprinkled a little, but the other one was not hit. They ran in separate directions. The mob waited for them to come back, but they did not. Sometime in the night, the elders got together and came back to the house. Then they left again for a while. But the elders kept coming back to the reservation until the church was built.

The whites just didn't want the Mormons to get established. Some Indian women had children by white men. They came in here to find the Indian women because they couldn't get out and ramble. That was the only reason the whites came in here.

They soon found that they couldn't keep the Indians from becoming Mormons. I don't think any of the whites around here belong. The whites still say things about the church that is not true. Polygamy has been done away with. They don't believe in the Prophet Joseph Smith; they say they would accept it if we would leave him out. They say the Bible is all we need.

In previous chapters we saw that the conversion of the Catawbas to Mormonism had several functions, one of which was to increase social distance between the Catawbas on the one hand, and whites, Negroes, and mestizos on the other.

Catawba historical beliefs reflect the bearing that their conversion to Mormonism had on social conflict. Before they became Mormons their conflict with whites was diffuse; after conversion conflict was focused into an "acceptable" area.

We have always had people to come into the Mormon church to try to convert people, but they have never succeeded. A Presbyterian couple came in, and somebody built a house for them. Somebody else built a building which was used for school and a Sunday preaching service. She taught school and regular

ministers came in to do the preaching on Sunday. The ones
who had gone to the Methodist church went into this church.

In 1912, the Baptists came in. The Mormon church shared
time with them. We had our meeting at three o'clock, and they
had theirs after that. The members that wanted to stay stayed,
and the rest went home. The ones who were Presbyterian went
to the Baptist church. It wasn't long before they joined the
Baptist church.

They didn't get enough members. They just had two families
who were drifting from church to church. Most of the Catawbas
joined the Mormon church because they felt it was the right
church. I don't know why the others didn't join. I don't know
why they drifted from church to church.

When the Catawbas became Mormons they also became
Christians. To the whites, however, they became the wrong
kind of Christians, and the whites were obligated to allocate
some of their missionary zeal toward converting Catawba
Mormons to a more acceptable kind of Christianity. Consequently, the conflict between whites and Catawbas became religious conflict, a form of conflict which is allowable,
being a part of the ideological fabric of American society.
By becoming Mormons the Catawbas put the whites in the
position of trying to persuade them to renounce Mormonism in favor of some other Christian religion.

Turning now to the positive side, we see that in belief as
well as in fact the Mormon religion provided the Catawbas
with an alternate value system, a source of self-esteem, and
a source of solidarity. Moreover, the Catawbas recognize a
positive social and cultural increment from Mormonism.

One of the biggest things to the Indians was the Mormon
church. The jobs were not as important as this. The church
gives them everything a young person needs. Good music, good
dress, and so forth. They teach square dancing, ballroom dancing, drama, sports, how to prepare for marriage.

As we shall presently see, the Catawbas see a discontinuity
in their past, and they largely attribute this discontinuity to
the influence of Mormonism. They see themselves as having
progressed in just the way that is prophesized in *The Book
of Mormon*.

When the Catawbas talk about their past, the one belief

that takes precedence over all the others is their belief in having changed. The Catawbas think of themselves as having progressed and as being progressive. They gave me many examples of their progress. One man said that several Mormon missionaries have told them that they are more advanced than other Indians. A Catawba woman whose grandson went to Chile as a Mormon missionary learned from him that the Chileans live today the way the Catawbas used to live on the Old Reservation.

Some of the older people told me about life as it used to be on the Old Reservation, contrasting it with the way things are now.

Yes a lot has gone on since 1943. Around 1930 to 1943 they had dances at home. That was back on the Old Reservation. Old and young would come, even children. A few of the little ones would dance. It was mostly square dances. They'd have a banjo, or a banjo and a guitar. Sometimes outside people came in and played. They had the dances to stay close to one another and for amusement. It would shift from one home to another.

They used to have a big dinner once a year—usually on the Fourth of July. They'd have beef soup and fish stew. Different ones would bring fried chicken. They would start cooking the beef and fish early in the morning. They would make lemonade. They didn't do it this year. They don't do it like they used to.

They used to announce it in church that someone needed a house. They built a lot of log houses. They were a lot more friendly towards each other. Now they are living far apart from each other and they are not as friendly. The branch president would announce it. A group of men would go work on the house and the women would do the cooking. After the house was built, there would be a big dance. They don't do this much now.

It looks to me that now the older ones just sit around. We have a lot of grandchildren who would rather stay home and watch TV than go play somewhere. I'll tell you one thing: some of the younger people are bad about taking an automobile ride on Sunday afternoon. All of this is since 1940.

The old man who told me about these changes rather sadly concluded that "everybody is in a hurry now."

The notion of change is even reflected in the fragmentary mythology that remains alive in Catawba memory. The most

widely known stories are about "little wild Indians," of whom
we have already seen an example.[3] Stories about little people
occur widely in the mythologies of the indigenous peoples
of the eastern United States, but for the Catawbas they were
symbols of Indianness (Witthoft and Hadlock 1946). It is
as if the Catawbas condense all their beliefs and feelings about
Indianness into a compact form—into small, darkish Indians
who roam abroad during the night. Here is another story
about them:

My mother always said that there were little wild Indians
who used to run around at night. If any of them touched your
children's clothes, your children would get sick. The old people
would not leave their children's clothes out at night. Even if
the children played in the dirt, they would brush away the
tracks. A wild Indian could tell all about the children from
the marks in the dirt. My grandmother said that they took her
brother away and kept him for a while. My mother really
believed in them. She never saw any of them, but she believed
in them. She said that they were all washed away in the 1916
flood.

When I was told about little wild Indians, the story
regularly ended with their being washed away in the 1916
flood. Each time I heard the story, I felt that the storyteller
was obliquely saying that the 1916 flood washed away the
Indianness of the Catawbas.

For some Catawbas this belief in having changed is reflected in a new self-image.

Some of the ones who live in Rock Hill don't think they're
Indians any more. When we terminated, the chief asked the
agent if they wouldn't be Indians any more after the sale of the
land. The agent said: "If you're not an Indian, what are you?"

Some of the Catawbas clearly regard themselves as being
white; some are perhaps not sure precisely what they are; and
some think of themselves as being Indians. But one indication
of change is evidenced by virtually all of them. When talking
about their history before 1940, and in some cases their more
recent history, they use "they" instead of "we." In their

---

3. Speck translates the Catawba word for these creatures as "mischievous
dwarfs" (Speck 1934:26-27).

choice of pronouns as well as in their beliefs, their remembered history has a break in it.

Opposed Folk Histories

To an outside observer the Catawbas and their white neighbors are heirs to a single history. More precisely, before Europeans began colonizing the southeastern United States, the ancestors of modern Catawbas and their white neighbors belonged to two different socio-cultural traditions; their histories were separate, distinct. But beginning with colonization and continuing to the present day, the Catawbas and the whites have increasingly participated in the same history, a unique succession of events occurring over the course of almost three centuries. At the time of colonization the Catawbas were a strategically located chiefdom, having cultural and social affiliations both with southeastern Indians and with Piedmont hill tribes. As colonization proceeded, the Catawbas were drawn into a plural South Carolina, becoming a socio-cultural segment in a society dominated by a white minority. However, as this plural society was transformed through industrialization and economic development, the Catawbas became increasingly assimilated into it, eventually terminating their Indian status with the Bureau of Indian Affairs.

However, even though the actions of the Catawbas and their white neighbors merge into a single objective history, this history has left incapsulated beliefs in the minds of Catawbas and whites that are only partially similar. The two sets of historical beliefs are similar in their choice of themes, both including themes accounting for (1) the origin of the Catawbas, (2) the traditional relationship between Catawbas and whites, and (3) a "principle" governing Catawba history from the colonial era to the present day. But given these similarities, the two sets of beliefs contain significant differences of detail.

Like societies with colonial experience in other parts of the world, the Catawbas and their white neighbors have opposed historical beliefs (Cf. Beattie 1964:24; 1962:11-24). By "opposed," I mean that the two sets of beliefs contain broad areas of agreement within which there are differences of detail, emphasis, and interpretation. From the standpoint of social structure and social history, these differences are as important as the similarities, perhaps more so.

Superficially, the similarities and differences between the two versions of Catawba history can be explained in terms of selective remembering. Neither the Catawbas nor the whites, for example, remember the composite nature of Catawba society in the eighteenth century, when the Catawba Nation was composed of refugees from a large number of shattered aboriginal societies. These complications have been obliterated from memory in favor of belief in descent from a single, discrete, nominate group. Moreover, in both versions historical time is telescoped into a small number of relatively timeless themes. Furthermore, the differences between the two sets of themes or beliefs are such that they flatter the self-image of those who hold them. Thus, the two versions of Catawba history are analogous to the memories that two individuals have of a mutual experience; they each remember the same experience but with inevitable differences caused by the experience being sifted through two different personalities.

This analogy from psychology is suggestive, but for a more adequate explanation of the similarities and differences we must examine the two sets of beliefs in their social context. The two sets of beliefs are held by two social categories of people who are members of a single society, a society whose plural structure has recently been transformed by economic development, and this above all accounts for the similarities. At the same time, however, the Catawbas and whites occupy *different* positions within this society, therefore having different values and interests. The whites, being dominant, have traditionally espoused rather conservative values and interests, generally emphasizing the status quo. In contrast the Catawbas, a minority group with rising expectations, have recently acquired "progressive" values and interests which co-exist with traditional values and interests. With these different values and interests in mind, let us now compare the two versions of Catawba history in some detail.

The two versions of Catawba history are most similar in accounting for the origin of the Catawbas. Both agree on the Catawbas being descended from stereotyped Indian ancestors, and both agree on the Catawbas having no Negro mixture.

This belief gives the Catawbas a clear place in the social universe. One slight difference in accounting for origin is that most of the Catawbas believe that they are descended from Lamanites; but even this belief is shared by whites who belong to the Mormon church. A further difference is that the whites appear to be rather more interested in the origin of the Catawbas than the Catawbas themselves are. This differential interest in the origin of the Catawbas is partly conditioned by white conservatism, by their interest in keeping Indians in their place. The lack of interest on the part of the Catawbas is conditioned, I think, by their putative descent from a known, documented, nominate Indian group. Parenthetically, this is precisely what is lacking among the mestizos who are actively trying to achieve Indian status. What the mestizos are trying to prove is for the Catawbas an accomplished fact.

The two versions of Catawba history are in essential agreement in accounting for the remote past, but when they account for events and conditions nearer to the present, they begin to diverge. In both belief systems, the traditional relationship between Catawbas and whites is represented in terms of friendship, but the nature of the friendship is depicted differently. According to the whites, the Catawbas were the best friends the colonists had: the Catawbas gave aid to the colonists spontaneously, as children of nature, asking little or nothing in return. The Catawbas agree that their ancestors were friendly towards the colonists. In fact, the Catawbas are quick to emphasize, they were too friendly; the whites not only took advantage of their friendship, but robbed them of their land and resources as well.

The significance of these different versions of Catawba-white friendship becomes clear when we see that they provided an ideological framework for "ordinary opposition," that is they were a set of beliefs which made it possible for conflict to occur within an overall structural constancy (Wilson 1954:125-132). For example, these beliefs made it possible for the Catawbas to visit the South Carolina legislature to solicit state aid on the grounds that the colonists had violated the friendship of their ancestors; consequently the whites owed them something. The whites, however, could rebut this argument on the grounds that the Catawbas lost their land through an inevitable evolutionary process, or on the grounds that the Catawbas were cheated out of their land by "white trash" who lived outside the moral universe of law-abiding white citizens. Thus, by virtue of the traditional friendship between Catawbas and whites being incapsulated in two different versions, it was possible for the Catawbas and whites to debate. It was an ideological framework within which the Catawbas could pursue their interests, and the whites could deny them, while, at the same time, leaving themselves a justification for giving aid to the Catawbas at a time that suited them.

The two versions of Catawba history are most dissimilar in characterizing the principle governing Catawba history from the Colonial era to the present. In the Catawba belief system their history has been governed by progress, which they largely attribute to the influence of Mormonism. Taking an opposite view, the whites believe that the Catawbas have declined. Once "great," the Catawbas are now a "disappearing nation." Moreover, the Mormon religion has no place in the white version of Catawba history. One white informant, who is supposed to be a local authority on the Catawbas, told me that the Catawbas have been Mormons for only ten or fifteen years. As we have seen, the first Catawbas were converted over seventy years ago.

The Catawbas and the whites are utterly at variance in characterizing the principle that has determined the "shape" of Catawba history. In part, this difference is probably caused by a difference in values, the whites taking a conservative view of things and the Catawbas a progressive view. Also, the difference is partly attributable to a difference in literacy: the whites, having a long literate tradition, are able to "freeze" the past; the Catawbas, having been literate for only fifty years or so, naturally emphasize events in the recent past.

To appreciate the social significance of folk history, we have to picture it not as a fragmentary recollection of a hazily remembered past, but as a part of the social context in which it occurs. Remembered history has been of use to both whites and Indians. The whites have used history to explain the social condition of the Catawbas in the recent past and to justify some of their transactions with them. Moreover, the whites value their own history, and their history articulates with the history of the Catawbas. Just after the Catawbas voted for termination, the York County Historical Commission decided to build a museum that "would be a handsome and fitting memorial to certain parts of Catawba culture."[4] The purpose of *Kah-Woh, Catawba* was to raise funds for this museum. While doing field work, I sometimes felt that some whites regarded the Catawbas almost as relics of their own history. If this impression is true, they must have been disconcerted by the Catawbas' determination to behave and live "like anybody else."

In the recent past the Catawbas have valued their history even more highly than the whites have valued theirs. They are quite aware that historical arguments have played an important role in winning rights and concessions from whites. On several occasions Catawbas told me that they "have a good history." They know that books and articles have been written about them, and they know that a photograph of one of their chiefs hangs in the Capitol at Washington. One Catawba told me that he feels the whites do not want a history of the Catawbas published because of the possibility that their title to the fifteen square miles held by the Catawbas before 1840 is of dubious legality.

Whether the Catawbas continue to value their history depends, I think, upon the degree to which they become assimilated in the larger society. I saw some evidence that they are beginning to devaluate their history. Several of them complained to me about whites who still expect them to live and behave like Indians. For example, when white tourists visit the reservation they usually ask where the chief lives. The Catawbas have no ready answer to this question because they have not had a formal chief since termination. As a further example, one man told me about an experience he had while serving food in a military mess hall:

> I knew a boy from Missouri in the service. He was shocked to see an Indian cooking and serving. In fact, he was afraid. He came up to me one day and said: "Chief (that's what

---

4. *Charlotte Observer*, Charlotte, North Carolina, September 18, 1960.

they called me), the schools have got us confused. We are taught that Indians are savage, but you are just like we are."

In conclusion, it can safely be said that assimilation of the Catawbas into the larger society will accelerate. As this occurs the Catawbas will become culturally, socially, and genetically "white," a process which the Catawbas fully anticipate. It is, after all, the fulfillment of a prophecy in *The Book of Mormon*. In a newspaper article, the last traditional chief is quoted as having said *"The Book of Mormon* promise to the Indians is coming true, and . . . the younger generation of Indians are now very light."[5] When the Catawbas succeed in becoming a "white and delightsome people," their folk history will no doubt assume a different form. Perhaps they will escape it entirely.

---

5. *Deseret Evening News*, Salt Lake City, Utah, May 1, 1954.

CHAPTER VII

History and Social Continuity

THE word "Catawba," as we have seen, has been a meaningful term since the latter part of the seventeenth century, designating for almost three hundred years a social "thing." The fundamental question which has guided this inquiry is what is the meaning of "Catawba," or to put it another way, what is the nature of the "thing" Catawba designates. There are a number of seemingly obvious answers to this question. For example, one common sense answer is that "Catawba" refers to the modern Catawba Indians who are descended from members of the Catawba Nation visited by John Lawson in 1700. But this answer, though having an appealing simplicity, omits many issues.

One of the fundamental axioms of common sense is that a word means today what it meant in the past. Without this axiomatic faith in a firm, relatively enduring nexus between a word and its meaning, our social universe would become unstructured and consequently unmanageable. At the same time, however, this axiom can lead people to see the world wrongly. It does so when it leads people to assume that "Catawba" retains something of the meaning it had in 1700, thus implying some kind of unity or continuity over the years.

It is of course true that from the standpoint of a detached observer one can see a strand of continuity in the social history of the Catawba Indians. That is, the Catawba Indians regarded as a social entity have occupied a social niche *vis a vis* whites from the time they were first contacted by traders until the recent past. During this time, however, far reaching changes have occurred both in Catawba society and in the

128

"surrounding" white society. Consequently, in order to conceptualize Catawba society as a continuous entity, we have to think of it as a continuously changing social structure within a social field that is likewise constantly changing. It is possible that a truly adequate theory of society would represent change in this way. That is, perhaps social structures are made up of parts which change not by leaps, as it were, but by slow shifts and accretions. If this is so, then the only sense in which "Catawba" denotes continuity is in the sense of continuous change.

Perhaps Catawba society has changed continuously, without leaps. However, because of the nature of the conceptual tools used in historical analysis, which are for the most part ordinary words and concepts used precisely, it is very difficult to conceptualize a continuous process and to represent it on paper. Consequently, even if social change is a continuous process, it is more convenient to conceptualize and represent it in discontinuous terms, i.e., as structure A at time 1 followed by a different structure B at time 2.

Moreover, one may argue on grounds more compelling than mere convenience that certain aspects of social change may be represented as being discontinuous. A social relationship (and the social structures made of such relationships) is made out of two kinds of materials: action and belief (Beattie 1964). Action, being the behavior of persons with respect to other persons, is a continuously variable, observable phenomenon. Belief, in contrast, being the means by which actors represent and idealize their social and cultural situation, is neither directly observable nor continuously variable.

Now, either of these two aspects or levels of a social structure may within limits change independently of the other. Moreover, the character of change at the two levels may differ. Gradual shifts and re-alignments may occur in the realm of action with few accompanying changes in the realm of belief. This may proceed to such a point that theory and practice no longer agree. Eventually, however, if the society is to make sense to the people who live in it, beliefs and values must be reinterpreted to fit the facts of life, and this reinterpretation may occur in a relatively short period of time. For example, we have seen that in the first half of this century several fundamental organizational changes occurred while the Catawbas were being assimilated into the larger society. Many of their beliefs and values, however, persisted even after they were obviously incompatible with these organizational changes. Then, in the years preceding termination these beliefs and values were reinterpreted in a rather dramatic fashion. The point is that these changes in fundamental social beliefs and values occurred in a short enough period of time to allow us to say that they constitute a discontinuity in Catawba society. Furthermore, we should recall that the Catawbas themselves explicitly recognize a discontinuity in their recent history. Thus, to speak of discontinuities in Catawba social history—their occupying different social positions at *different* times—involves more than mere analytical convenience.

Ignoring the transitional periods in Catawba history, "Catawba" has been used to designate three distinctly different social entities in three periods of time: (1) an aboriginal Southern chiefdom, (2) a socio-cultural section in a plural society, and (3) a highly assimilated ethnic group in a modern industrial society. We now see that this inquiry into a question with an "obvious" answer turns out to require an answer that is not at all obvious. Indeed, the referents of "Catawba" are objectively so different, it is little short of astonishing that a single word has been used to refer to all of them. The reason for this semantic oddity lies, of course, in the fact that social change is slow with respect to the lifespan of individuals. Societies, as S. F. Nadel (1951:82-83) has noted, appear to be concrete "things" because they have names, and these names are borne by successive generations.

Nadel has emphasized the importance of names in making social groups visible and in expressing an awareness of belonging, e.g., "I am a Catawba." Along with this, I would emphasize the importance of names in social continuity. Groups change, but people continue calling them by the same name. This calls to mind E. E. Evans-Pritchard's burlesque of the analogy social scientists make between a society and an organism: "But a society, however defined, in no way resembles a horse, and, mercifully, horses remain horses—at least they have done so in historic times—and do not turn into elephants or pigs, whereas a society may change from one type to another, sometimes with great suddenness and violence" (1962:55). In the realm of human society, horses *do* change into elephants or pigs, but people, through their peculiar ability to use categories, continue to call them horses, and sometimes they continue to think they are horses.

Bibliography

Adair, James. 1930. *Adair's History of the American Indians* (Johnson City, Tennessee: Watauga Press).

Alden, John Richard. 1944. *John Stuart and the Southern Frontier* (Ann Arbor: University of Michigan Press).

Allen, Louis. 1931. Siouan and Iroquoian. *International Journal of American Linguistics* 6:185-193.

Alvord, Clarence Walworth and Lee Bigood. 1912. *The First Explorations of the Trans-Allegheny Region by the Virginians, 1650-1674* (Cleveland, Ohio: Arthur H. Clark Company).

Anonymous. 1897. The Catawba Tribe of Indians. Senate Document No. 144, 54th Congress, 2nd Session (February 3, 1897).

Anonymous. 1906. A Treaty Between Virginia and the Catawbas and Cherokees, 1756. *Virginia Magazine of History and Biography* 13:225-264.

Bartram, William. n.d. *Travels of William Bartram*, Mark Van Doren, ed. (New York: Dover Publications).

Beattie, John. 1960. *Bunyoro: An African Kingdom* (New York: Holt, Rinehart and Winston).

1964. *Other Cultures: Aims, Methods and Achievements in Social Anthropology* (New York: The Free Press of Glencoe).

Berry, Brewton. 1945. The Mestizos of South Carolina. *American Journal of Sociology* 51:34-41.

1963. *Almost White* (New York: Macmillan Company).

Binford, Lewis R. 1959. Comments on the 'Siouan Problem'. *Ethnohistory* 6:28-41.

1967. An Ethnohistory of the Nottoway, Meherrin and Weanock Indians of Southeastern Virginia, *Ethnohistory* 14:104-218.

Bland, Edward. 1912. The Discovery of New Brittaine. In Clarence Walworth Alvord and Lee Bigood, *The First Explorations of the Trans-Allegheny Region by the Virginians, 1650-1674* (Cleveland, Ohio: Arthur H. Clark Company), pp. 109-130.

Bradford, W. R. c. 1944. The Catawba Indians of South Carolina, printed under the direction of the South Carolina Senate (Columbia, South Carolina: Farrell Printing Company).

Brevard, Joseph. 1814. *An Alphabetical Digest of the Public Statute Laws of South Carolina,* 3 Vols. (Charleston, South Carolina: John Hall).

Brown, Douglas Summers. 1953. *A City Without Cobwebs* (Columbia: University of South Carolina Press).
1966. *The Catawba Indians: The People of the River* (Columbia: University of South Carolina Press).

Brown, Ralph H. 1943. *Mirror for Americans: Likeness of the Eastern Seaboard, 1810,* American Geographical Society, Special Publication No. 27 (New York: George Grady Press).

Byrd, William. 1929. *Histories of the Dividing Line Betwixt Virginia and North Carolina* (Raleigh: North Carolina Historical Commission).

Caldwell, Joseph R. 1952. The Archaeology of Eastern Georgia and South Carolina. In *Archaeology of Eastern United States,* James B. Griffin, ed. (Chicago: The University of Chicago Press), pp. 312-321.

Carstens, Peter. 1966. *The Social Structure of a Cape Coloured Reserve* (Cape Town: Oxford University Press).

Carver, John A. Jr. 1961. "Notice of Final Membership Roll of the Catawba Indian Tribe of South Carolina," mimeographed document (Washington, D. C.: United States Department of the Interior, Office of the Secretary).

Coe, Joffre Lanning. 1952. The Cultural Sequence of the Carolina Piedmont. In *Archaeology of Eastern United States,* James B. Griffin, ed. (Chicago: University of Chicago Press), pp. 301-311.
1961. Cherokee Archaeology. In *Symposium on Cherokee and Iroquois Cultures,* William N. Fenton and John Gulick, eds. Smithsonian Institution, Bureau of American Ethnology, Bulletin No. 180 (Washington, D. C.: U. S. Government Printing Office), pp. 53-60.
1964. *The Formative Cultures of the Carolina Piedmont.* Transactions of the American Philosophical Society, Vol. 54, Part 5 (Philadelphia: American Philosophical Society).

Covington, James W. 1954. Proposed Catawba Indian Removal, 1848. *South Carolina Historical and Genealogical Magazine* 54:42-47.

Crane, Verner W. 1959. *The Southern Frontier: 1670-1732*

(Ann Arbor: Ann Arbor Paperbacks, University of Michigan Press).

Cumming, William Patterson. 1958. *The Southeast in Early Maps* (Princeton, N. J.: Princeton University Press).

Cunnison, Ian. 1951. *History on the Luapula: An Essay on the Historical Notions of a Central African Tribe*, Rhodes-Livingstone Papers No. 21 (Cape Town, London, New York: Oxford University Press).

Elkins, Stanley M. 1963. *Slavery: A Problem in American Institutional and Intellectual Life* (New York: Grosset & Dunlap, The Universal Library).

Evans-Pritchard, E. E. 1962a. Social Anthropology: Past and Present. In *Essays in Social Anthropology* (London: Faber and Faber), pp. 13-28.

1962b. Anthropology and History. In *Essays in Social Anthropology* (London: Faber and Faber), pp. 46-65.

Fallam, Robert. 1912. The Expedition of Batts and Fallam. In Clarence Walworth Alvord and Lee Bigood, *The First Explorations of the Trans-Allegheny Region by the Virginians, 1650-1674* (Cleveland, Ohio: Arthur B. Clark Company), pp. 181-195.

Fewkes, Vladimir J. 1944. Catawba Pottery-Making, With Notes on Pamunkey Pottery-Making, Cherokee Pottery-Making, and Coiling. *Proceedings of the American Philosophical Society* 88:69-124.

Frachtenberg, Leo J. 1913. Contributions to a Tutelo Vocabulary. *American Anthropologist* 15:477-479.

Furnivall, J. S. 1948. *Colonial Policy and Practice* (London: Cambridge University Press).

Gallatin, Albert. 1836. A Synopsis of the Indian Tribes within the United States East of the Rocky Mountains. Transactions and Collections of the American Antiquarian Society. *Archaeologia Americana* 2:1-422.

Gatschet, Albert S. 1900. Grammatic Sketch of the Catawba Language. *American Anthropologist* 2:527-549.

1902. Onomatology of the Catawba River Basin. *American Anthropologist* 4:52-56.

Gearing, Fred. 1962. *Priests and Warriors: Social Structures for Cherokee Politics in the 18th Century*. American Anthropological Association Memoir No. 93, Vol. 64, No. 5, Part 2.

Gilbert, William H. Jr. 1946. Memorandum Concerning the Characteristics of the Larger Mixed-Blood Racial Islands of the Eastern United States. *Social Forces* 24:438-447.

1949. Surviving Indian Groups of the Eastern United States. *Smithsonian Report for 1948* (Washington, D. C.: U. S. Government Printing Office), pp. 407-438.

Glen, James. 1951. A Description of South Carolina. In *Colonial South Carolina: Two Contemporary Descriptions*, Chapman Milling, ed. (Columbia: University of South Carolina Press).

Goldschmidt, Arthur. 1963. The Development of the U. S. South. *Scientific American* 209:224-232.

Gregg, Alexander. 1867. *History of the Old Cheraws* (New York: Richardson and Company).

Griffin, James B. 1952. Culture Periods in Eastern United States Archaeology. In *Archaeology of Eastern United States*, James B. Griffin, ed. (Chicago: University of Chicago Press), pp. 352-364.

Hale, Horatio. 1883. The Tutelo Tribe and Language. *Proceedings of the American Philosophical Society* 21:1-47.

Hallowell, A. Irving. 1957. The Impact of the American Indian on American Culture. *American Anthropologist* 59:201-217.

Harrington, M. R. 1908. Catawba Potters and their Work. *American Anthropologist* 10:399-407.

Harrison, Fairfax. 1922. Western Explorations in Virginia Between Lederer and Spotswood. *Virginia Magazine of History and Biography* 30:323-340.

Hicks, George L. 1964. Catawba Acculturation and the Ideology of Race. In *Symposium on New Approaches to the Study of Religion*, Melford E. Spiro, ed. American Ethnological Society (Seattle: University of Washington Press), pp. 116-124.

Holman, C. Hugh. 1961. "Introduction," to William Gilmore Simms, *The Yemassee: A Romance of Carolina* (Boston: Houghton Mifflin Company), pp. vii-xx.

Hudson, Charles. 1966. Folk History and Ethnohistory. *Ethnohistory* 13:52-70.

Jacobs, Wilbur R. (ed). *Indians of the Southern Frontier: The Edmond Atkin Report and Plan of 1755* (Columbia: University of South Carolina Press).

Jenson, Andrew. 1941. *Encyclopedic History of the Church of Jesus Christ of Latter-day Saints* (Salt Lake City, Utah: Deseret News Publishing Company).

Kirkland, Thomas J. and Robert M. Kennedy. 1905. *Historic Camden*, Part I (Columbia, South Carolina: The State Company).

Klingberg, Frank J. (ed). 1956. *The Carolina Chronicle of*

Dr. Francis Le Jau, 1706-1717. University of California Publications in History, Vol. 53 (Berkeley: University of California Press).

Kroeber, Alfred L. 1939. *Cultural and Natural Areas of Native North America.* University of California Publications in American Archaeology and Ethnology, Vol. 38 (Berkeley: University of California Press).

Lawson, John. 1960. *Lawson's History of North Carolina,* 3rd edition (Richmond, Virginia: Garrett and Massie, Publishers).

Lederer, John. 1912. The Discoveries of John Lederer. In Clarence Walworth Alvord and Lee Bigood (eds.), *The First Explorations of the Trans-Allegheny Region by the Virginians, 1650-1674* (Cleveland, Ohio: Arthur H. Clark Company), pp. 131-171.

Lieber, Oscar M. 1858. Vocabulary of the Catawba Language, with some Remarks on its Grammar Construction and Pronunciation. *Collections of the South Carolina Historical Society,* Vol. 2. (Charleston, South Carolina: James and Williams, Printers), pp. 327-342.

Lewis, Ernest. 1951. "The Sara Indians, 1540-1768: An Ethno-Archaeological Study." Unpublished Master's thesis, University of North Carolina.

Long, William I. 1960. "Kah-Woh, Catawba: A Drama of the Catawba Indians of South Carolina and the White People Closely Associated with Them, from 1750-1791," mimeographed document.

Marais, J. S. 1962. *The Cape Coloured People, 1652-1937* (Johannesburg: Witwaterstrand University Press), first published 1939.

Mason, Carol Irwin. 1963. A Reconsideration of the Westo-Yuchi Identification. *American Anthropologist* 65:1342-1346.

Miller, Carl F. 1957. "Reevaluation of the Eastern Siouan Problem with Particular Emphasis on the Virginian Branches— the Occaneechi, the Saponi, and the Tutelo," Smithsonian Institute, Bureau of American Ethnology, Bulletin No. 164, Anthropological Paper No. 52 (Washington, D. C.: U. S. Government Printing Office), pp. 115-211.

McDowell, W. L. (ed.). 1955. *Journals of the Commissions of the Indian Trade, September 20, 1710-August 1718,* Colonial Records of South Carolina, Columbia, South Carolina: State Commercial Printing Company).

Meriwether, Robert L. 1940. *The Expansion of South Carolina, 1729-1765* (Kingsport, Tennessee: Southern Publishers, Inc.).

Milligen-Johnston, George. 1951. A Short Description of the Province of South Carolina. In *Colonial South Carolina: Two Contemporary Descriptions*, Chapman J. Milling, ed. (Columbia: University of South Carolina Press).

Milling, Chapman J. 1940. *Red Carolinians* (Chapel Hill: University of North Carolina Press).

Mills, Robert. 1825. *Statistics of South Carolina* (Charleston, South Carolina: Published by Hurlbut and Lloyd).

Mooney, James. 1894. *The Siouan Tribes of the East*. Bulletin of the Bureau of American Ethnology, No. 22 (Washington, D. C.: U. S. Government Printing Office).

—— 1900. *Myths of the Cherokee*. Smithsonian Institution, Bureau of American Ethnology, 19th Annual Report, Part I (Washington, D. C.: U. S. Government Printing Office).

Murphy, Christopher and Charles Hudson. 1968. On the Problem of Intensive Agriculture in the Aboriginal Southeastern United States. *Working Papers in Sociology and Anthropology* (Department of Sociology and Anthropology, University of Georgia), 2:24-34.

Myer, William E. 1928. "Indian Trails of the Southeast" Smithsonian Institution, Bureau of American Ethnology, 42nd Annual Report (Washington, D. C.: U. S. Government Printing Office), pp. 725-857.

Nadel, S. F. 1951. *The Foundations of Social Anthropology* (London: Cohen and West, Ltd.).

Neil, Franklin W. 1932. Virginia and the Cherokee Indian Trade, 1673-1752. *The East Tennessee Historical Society's Publications* 4:3-21.

O'Dea, Thomas F. 1957. *The Mormons* (Chicago: University of Chicago Press).

Olmsted, Frederick Law. 1959. *The Slave States* (New York: Capricorn Books).

Rivers, William James. 1885. *A Chapter in the Colonial History of the Carolinas* (Baltimore: John Murphy and Company, Inc.).

Rothrock, Mary U. 1929. Carolina Traders Among the Overhill Cherokees, 1690-1760. *The East Tennessee Historical Society's Publications* 1:3-18.

Salley, Alexander S. Jr. (ed.). 1911. *Narratives of Early Carolina, 1650-1708* (New York: Charles Scribner's Sons).

Salley, A. S. 1929. "The Boundary Line Between North Carolina and South Carolina," Bulletin of the Historical Commission of South Carolina, No. 10 (Columbia, South Carolina: The State Company).

1932. "President Washington's Tour through South Carolina in 1791," Bulletin of the Historical Commission of South Carolina, No. 12 (Columbia, South Carolina: The State Company).

Sapir, Edward. 1913. A Tutelo Vocabulary. *American Anthropologist* 15:295-297.

1951. Time Perspective in Aboriginal American Culture: A Study in Method. In *Selected Writings of Edward Sapir*, David G. Mandelbaum, ed. (Berkeley and Los Angeles: University of California Press), pp. 389-462.

Scaife, Lewis H. 1896. "History and Condition of the Catawba Indians of South Carolina." (Philadelphia, Pennsylvania: Office of the Indian Rights Association).

Service, Elman R. 1962. *Primitive Social Organization* (New York: Random House).

Siebert, Frank T. Jr. 1945. Linguistic Classification of Catawba. *International Journal of American Linguistics* 11:100-104, 211-218.

Simms, William Gilmore. n.d. *The Wigwam and the Cabin* (Atlanta, Georgia: The Martin and Hoyt Company).

Smith, M. G. 1960. Social and Cultural Pluralism. In Vera Rubin (ed.), *Social and Cultural Pluralism in the Caribbean*, Annals of the New York Academy of Sciences 83:763-777.

Smyth, John Ferdinand D. 1784. *A Tour in the United States*, 2 Vols. (Dublin: Printed by G. Perrin).

Speck, Frank G. 1913. Some Catawba Texts and Folklore. *Journal of American Folklore* 26:319-330.

1934. *Catawba Texts*. Columbia University Contributions to Anthropology, Vol. 24 (New York: Columbia University Press).

1935. Siouan Tribes of the Carolinas as Known from Catawba, Tutelo, and Documentary Sources. *American Anthropologist* 37:201-225.

1937. Catawba Medicines and Curative Practices. In *Twenty-Fifth Anniversary Studies: Philadelphia Anthropological Society*, D. S. Davidson, ed. (Pittsburg: University of Pittsburg Press).

1938a. Question of Matrilineal Descent in the Southeastern Siouan Area. *American Anthropologist* 40:1-12.

1938b. The Cane Blowgun in Catawba and Southeastern Ethnology, *American Anthropologist* 40:198-204.

1939a. Catawba Religious Beliefs, Mortuary Customs, and Dances. *Primitive Man* 12:21-57.

1939b. The Catawba Nation and its Neighbors. *North Carolina Historical Review* 16:404-417.

1944a. Catawba Games and Amusements. *Primitive Man* 17:19-28.

1944b. Catawba Herbals and Curative Practices. *Journal of American Folklore* 57:37-50.

1946a. *Catawba Hunting, Trapping, and Fishing* (Philadelphia, Pennsylvania: University of Pennsylvania Museum).

1946b. Catawba Texts. *International Journal of American Linguistics* 12:64-67.

1946c. Ethnoherpetology of the Catawba and Cherokee Indians. *Journal of the Washington Academy of Science* 36:355-360.

1947. Catawba Folk Tales from Chief Sam Blue. *Journal American Folklore* 60:79-84.

Speck, Frank G. and C. E. Schaeffer. 1924. Catawba Kinship and Social Organization with a Resume of Tutelo Kinship Terms. *American Anthropologist* 44:555-575.

Sturtevant, William C. 1958. Siouan Languages in the East. *American Anthropologist* 60:738-743.

1962. Spanish-Indian Relations in Southeastern North America. *Ethnohistory* 9:41-94.

Swanton, John R. 1918. Catawba Notes. *Journal of the Washington Academy of Science* 8:623-629.

1922. *Early History of the Creek Indians and their Neighbors.* Smithsonian Institution, Bureau of American Ethnology Bulletin No. 73 (Washington, D. C.: U. S. Government Printing Office).

1936. Early History of the Eastern Siouan Tribes. In *Essays in Anthropology Presented to A. L. Kroeber*, R. H. Lowie, ed. (Berkeley: University of California Press), pp. 371-381.

1940. The First Description of an Indian Tribe in the Territory of the Present United States. In *Studies for William A. Read* (Baton Rouge: Louisiana State University Press), pp. 326-338.

1946. *The Indians of the Southeastern United States.* Smithsonian Institution, Bureau of American Ethnology, Bulletin No. 137 (Washington, D. C.: U. S. Government Printing Office).

Tang, Anthony M. 1958. *Economic Development in the Southern Piedmont, 1860-1950* (Chapel Hill: University of North Carolina Press).

Vance, Rupert B. 1932. *Human Geography of the South* (Chapel Hill: University of North Carolina Press).

Visher, Stephen Sargent. 1954. *Climatic Atlas of the United States* (Cambridge: Harvard University Press).

Voegelin, C. F. 1941. Internal Relationships of Siouan Languages. *American Anthropologist* 43:246-249.

Wallace, David Duncan. 1951. *South Carolina: A Short History, 1520-1948* (Chapel Hill: University of North Carolina Press).

Wilson, Godfrey and Monica Wilson. 1954. *The Analysis of Social Change* (Cambridge: The University Press).

Witthoft, John and Wendell S. Hadlock. 1946. Cherokee-Iroquois Little People. *Journal of American Folklore* 59:413-420.

Wood, Abraham. 1912. The Journeys of Needham and Arthur. In Clarence Walworth Alvord and Lee Bigood, *The First Explorations of the Trans-Allegheny Region by the Virginians, 1650-1674* (Cleveland, Ohio: Arthur H. Clark Company), pp. 210-226.

Wraxall, Peter. 1915. *An Abridgement of the Indian Affairs*, Charles Howard McIlwain (ed.). Harvard Historical Studies, Vol. 21 (Cambridge: Harvard University Press).

Index

Adshusheer Indians, 7

Agriculture: before contact, 12-13, 17, 20-21; as practiced by white yeomen, 54-55; as practiced by modern Catawbas, 63n, 71, 74-75, 76, 85, 88, 108

Appalachian Mountains, 11

Atlantic Coastal Plain, 11, 18-20

Backhook Indians, 7

Badin cultural complex, 12

Black Code, 69

Black. *See* Negroes

Blue, Chief. *See* Chief Blue

Bureau of Indian Affairs: aid to Catawbas, 65, 86-87, 90, 100; conflict with Catawbas, 91; institutes tribal council, 96; role in termination, 101

Cape Fear Indians, 7, 15, 47

Catawba language: extinction, 3, 66, 77, 107; classified, 6, 8; dialects, 28, 47

Cherokee Indians: location 6, 9, 13-14; ancestors, 12, 27; as southern chiefdom, 23; English trade with, 24, 31, 37-38, 45; and Catawbas, 26, 27-28, 38, 65-66, 114, 115; identified as Tomahittans, 37; affiliations with other Indians, 38; feared by Whites, 43-44, 49; and French and Indian War, 49; attended Augusta Congress, 50; and Mormonism, 78

Cherokee War, 49, 50, 51

Chief Blue, 74, 107-108, 112-113

Civil War, 67, 111

Congaree Indians: and Whites, 1, 34, 42; classified, 7, 15; and Catawbas, 47-48

Creek Indians: location, 6, 9; ancestors, 12, 27; and English, 24, 43-44; attend Augusta Congress, 50

Cusabo Indians, 23, 42

Eastern Siouans, 5-9, 15, 38, 114

Education, of Catawbas, 83, 84, 86, 87

Eno Indians, 7, 47

Esaw Indians, 2, 26, 28

Flat Heads, 26-27

Folk history, 4, 105, 125

Fort Mill, South Carolina, 78, 81

French and Indian War, 49, 50, 51

Glen, James, 47, 48n, 49

Head deformation, 26-27

Hill tribes: description, 12-13, 17; territory of, 14; cultural development, 15-16; agriculture, 20-21; social organization, 23-26; English trade with, 32

Hook Indians, 7

Hale, Horatio, 6

Intermarriage, 69-70, 83, 88-89, 93, 101

Keyauwee Indians, 7, 26

Ku Klux Klan, 69-70

Manahoac Indians, 7-8

Meipontsky Indians, 7

Mestizos, 67, 70-71, 116

Mohetan Indians, 7, 32

Monacan Indians, 7-8, 32

Mormonism: conversion of Catawbas, 53, 77-80; church's role in settling disputes, 94; land given to church, 102; Rock Hill congregation divided, 103-104; in Catawba folk history, 114, 117-120, 125; prophecy fulfilled, 127

141